MADE IN ASIAN AMERICA

A HISTORY FOR YOUNG PEOPLE

ALSO BY ERIKA LEE

Angel Island: Immigrant Gateway to America (with Judy Yung)
The Making of Asian America: A History
*America for Americans: A History of Xenophobia in the
United States*

ALSO BY CHRISTINA SOONTORNVAT

*All Thirteen: The Incredible Cave Rescue
of the Thai Boys' Soccer Team*
A Life of Service: The Story of Senator Tammy Duckworth
The Last Mapmaker

MADE IN ASIAN AMERICA

A HISTORY FOR YOUNG PEOPLE

ERIKA LEE &
CHRISTINA SOONTORNVAT

Quill Tree Books
An Imprint of HarperCollinsPublishers

Quill Tree Books is an imprint of HarperCollins Publishers.

This book has been adapted from *The Making of Asian America:
A History* by Erika Lee (Simon & Schuster, 2015).

Library of Congress Control Number: 2023942526
ISBN 978-0-06-324293-7

Typography by Kathy H. Lam
24 25 26 27 28 LBC 5 4 3 2 1
First Edition

TO ALL THE YOUNG PEOPLE
WORKING TO CREATE A BETTER WORLD
FOR ALL OF US.

TABLE OF CONTENTS

INTRODUCTION

There is a saying: "History repeats itself."

People use it all the time to explain why or how something might happen over and over again.

But is it true?

When it comes to the history of Asian Americans, most people were never taught enough in school to know the answer. Some students *might* have learned how Chinese immigrant workers helped to build the transcontinental railroad. Or *maybe* they have read about the incarceration of Japanese Americans during World War II. But that's usually about it.

Eighteen-year-old Soorya "Rio" Baliga is one of those students who never learned about Asian American history in her classes. It made her feel like she was left out of history: "There was essentially implicit messaging on the part of the public school system telling me 'you don't matter; these white figures are the people worth learning about.' That's harmful and it makes you devalue yourself in a way."

Seventeen-year-old Russell Fan had to learn about Asian American heroes on his own. In school, he was never taught about Patsy Mink, the first woman of color elected to Congress, or labor organizing legend Larry Itliong. It was frustrating that he had to wait so long. He felt that all young people deserved to know about these inspiring Americans. They needed to see that Asian Americans weren't perpetual foreigners, but a vital and vibrant part of the fabric of the country. If that happened, surely it would help in the fight against the racism that he and so many other young Asian Americans were experiencing.

College student Gabriella Son was one of many students testifying during a rally and press conference at the New Jersey State House in Trenton in December 2021, calling for the teaching of Asian American and Pacific Islander history in schools.

Christina Huang can remember being the target of racism when she was in the first grade. The school bus had pulled up in front of her house, where her grandmother was outside doing her exercises. Christina's classmates teased her, called her names, and stretched the corners of their eyes, mocking her. That moment didn't destroy

Christina's pride in who she was, but it was deeply painful.

Ten-year-old Bryan Zhao was sitting on his trampoline in his backyard when a white man walked up to the fence. He looked Bryan in the eye, bent down, and spat onto the ground. Bryan didn't say anything. It had happened too fast to process. But he knew what it was. That man had meant to send a message to Bryan: a message of racism and hate.

Bryan's encounter happened in 2020, during the rise of the global COVID-19 pandemic. Lawmakers and media personalities were using racist terms to describe the virus and blame Chinese people for the spread of the disease. The president of the United States at the time even called it "the Chinese virus." New Jersey high school junior Kyler Zhou was at soccer practice when he was told that he and "his people" had caused the pandemic. All over the country, Asian Americans were experiencing a rise in racist and violent encounters.

Slurs were hurled at Asian Americans in the street: "This pandemic wouldn't have happened if you stayed in your country where you belong!" or "You brought the virus on purpose!" A majority (68 percent) of the attacks were directed at females. Children and the elderly were other targets. Harassers seemed to be singling out the most vulnerable. In San Francisco on January 28, 2021, an eighty-four-year-old Thai American grandfather named Vicha Ratanapakdee was shoved to the ground by a stranger. He died of his injuries. Vicha was one of many elderly Asian Americans who were assaulted.

And then, on March 6, 2021, an armed gunman entered three

Asian-owned businesses in Atlanta, Georgia, and opened fire, killing eight people. Six of them were Asian American women. The shooter had stated that he wanted to "kill all Asians." Less than a month later, four Sikh American warehouse workers were targeted, shot, and killed in Indianapolis.

These mass shootings rocked the Asian American community. There was a simultaneous feeling of *this can't be happening in the year 2021*, along with the chilling suspicion that *we have been here before.*

People gather to protest at the "Rally Against Hate" in Chinatown on March 21, 2021, in New York City.

The rise in hate crimes against Asian Americans in the early 2020s felt connected to those individual, personal stories of feeling "othered," like those of Bryan and Christina. It felt connected to their parents' and grandparents' stories, and it felt connected to the fragments of Asian American history that they did know.

Russell, Rio, Kyler, Bryan, and Christina felt they had to do something. Staying silent or accepting the violence was not an option. It was the height of the pandemic, which meant that all over the country, Americans were in physical isolation. Even so, the teenagers used the tools they had to find their voices and to find each other.

Rio wrote articles about discrimination and COVID-19. Kyler started a magazine about Asian American issues called *Hear Our Voices*. At first, it was just him and two other friends writing. Within a year and a half, the magazine had a staff of twenty-six and over 15,000 readers. Russell founded a group in his New Jersey hometown called the Livingston AAPI Youth Alliance. Members of the Alliance, along with other Asian American youth like Christina, Rio, Kyler, and Bryan, started working with parents, teachers, and other advocates to make schools require Asian American and Pacific Islander history. They all believed that learning about the history of Asian Americans was necessary to understand what was happening to Asian Americans today.

These young activists joined the long legacy of Asian Americans who have stood up, spoken out, and worked alongside others to make America live up to its ideals as a nation of justice, equality, and freedom.

Asian American history is not made up of one single story. It's many. And it's a story that you have to know if you want to understand the history of America.

It begins centuries before America even existed as a nation. It is connected to the histories of Western exploration, conquest, and colonialism in Asia and beyond. It's a story of migration; of people and families crossing the Pacific Ocean in search of new beginnings and opportunities or to escape hunger, poverty, and persecution.

It is also the story of race and racism. Of being unjustly categorized along with Native Americans and African Americans as inferior, dangerous, uncivilized, and unfit to become citizens. Of being segregated and prevented from attending certain schools, working in certain jobs, and living in particular neighborhoods. Of being labeled an immigrant invasion and national security threat and banned, deported, driven out, incarcerated, and spied upon. Of being blamed for bringing diseases into the country.

But it is also a story of heroism and bravery. Of fighting for equality in the courts, on the streets, in the schools, and in solidarity with others doing the same.

Does history repeat itself?

To know the answer, you first have to know the history. . . .

WHO ARE ASIAN AMERICANS?

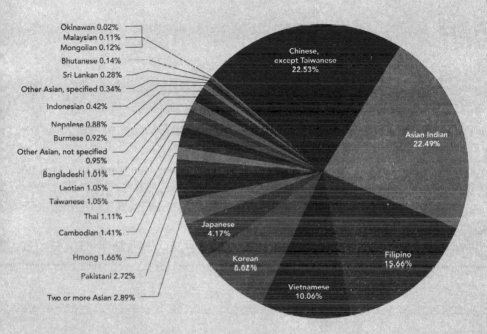

Okinawan 0.02%
Malaysian 0.11%
Mongolian 0.12%
Bhutanese 0.14%
Sri Lankan 0.28%
Other Asian, specified 0.34%
Indonesian 0.42%
Nepalese 0.88%
Burmese 0.92%
Other Asian, not specified 0.95%
Bangladeshi 1.01%
Laotian 1.05%
Taiwanese 1.05%
Thai 1.11%
Cambodian 1.41%
Hmong 1.66%
Pakistani 2.72%
Two or more Asian 2.89%

Chinese, except Taiwanese 22.53%
Asian Indian 22.49%
Filipino 15.66%
Vietnamese 10.06%
Korean 8.02%
Japanese 4.17%

Asian Americans in the US (data from the US Census, 2016–2020).

Asian Americans are people who can trace their roots to countries throughout East Asia, South Asia, and Southeast Asia. Before World War II, Chinese and Japanese people made up the biggest Asian American communities in the US, but South Asians, Koreans, and Filipinos also came in large numbers. After US immigration laws changed in 1965, an even greater diversity of Asian immigrants came from India, Pakistan, Bangladesh, Hong Kong, Taiwan,

Vietnam, Cambodia, Laos, and other nations.

Asian Americans are an incredibly diverse group, representing different religions, languages, societal status, and generations. There is no single Asian American story, though there are many similarities and connections.

The US Census uses the term "Asian American Pacific Islander," or AAPI, to also refer to those who trace their heritage to the Indigenous peoples of the Micronesian, Melanesian, and Polynesian islands, including Native Hawaiians. While Pacific Islanders, Kānaka Maoli (Indigenous Hawaiian people), and Asian Americans do have many things in common, there are also important differences that can get lost when the groups are combined. The histories of Pacific Islander Americans and Native Hawaiians are complex, rich, and deserving of their own treatment, and so they are not included in this book.

Today, Asian Americans make up 7 percent of the US population and are the fastest growing group in the United States. They are a vital part of America's future, and with growing numbers comes growing political power, growing responsibility, and a desire to know and understand their full history.

COLUMBUS'S MISTAKE

Some mistakes are so big, they make history.

When the Spanish explorer Christopher Columbus stepped off his ship and set foot on the Caribbean island of Guanahani in 1492, he was sure that he had achieved his life's mission. This achievement would make him famous. It would bring glory to his king and queen. This moment would be recorded in history books, because this place that he had landed . . . was Asia.

At least, it was *supposed* to be Asia.

Europeans, going all the way back to the ancient Greeks, had long been fascinated with Asia. And not necessarily in a good way. They viewed the lands of "the East" as their polar opposite. For Europeans, the West was known. The East was mysterious. Europe was "civilized." Asia was wild and barbaric. Europe was strong. Asia was weak, inferior, and ready to be conquered. Most of all: Asia was full of riches, ripe for the taking.

A late sixteenth-century engraving of Christopher Columbus arriving in the "New World" depicted the arrival of Spanish colonizers as a peaceful and welcomed event that brought Christianity to the "uncivilized" Indigenous peoples they met.

These ideas were spread by European merchants and travel writers who journeyed to Asia and spun fantastic tales of their eastern travels. One of the most influential travel writers of the Middle Ages was a man named Marco Polo. In the 1200s, his popular book about his journeys in the Middle East and Asia described unicorns, exotic customs, and mountain streams flowing with diamonds, as well as "heathens" who could be converted to Christianity. His writings helped to stoke a rising European hunger for all things from the "Orient," especially spices, silks, and sugar.

Whoever could figure out how to fulfill that demand stood to make a lot of money. The Portuguese sailor Vasco da Gama found a way to reach Asia by sailing around the coast of Africa. When he returned home, he sold the cargo in the belly of his ship for *six times* the price he paid for it. Clearly, this trade route was worth more than gold, and the Portuguese weren't going to let anyone else have it. At one point, Portugal claimed that all of the Indian Ocean belonged to them, and they prevented ships from other countries from sailing there to trade. This might seem unfair, but according to the Portuguese, it was *Finders Keepers*.

That meant that if other European countries, like Spain, wanted to reach the riches of the Orient, they were going to have to find another way to get there.

Enter Christopher Columbus.

Inspired by Marco Polo's writings, Columbus set off across the Atlantic Ocean to find a new route to Asia and claim it for Spain. But when his ships landed in the Caribbean in 1492, something seemed a little . . . odd.

Where were the spice markets that Marco Polo had written about? Where were the gold-roofed buildings? Asia wasn't supposed to look like this.

Unfazed, he wrote to the king and queen of Spain, telling them that these "new lands" were full of boundless wealth and native people who would be easy to convert to Christianity and enslave. Best of all, Spain could claim it all for themselves, because *Finders Keepers*.

Of course, Christopher Columbus hadn't found Asia. And of course, he hadn't *found* the Americas, either. What would eventually be known as North and South America had been populated for at least 15,000 years. The population of both continents before Columbus arrived was about 90 million. Indigenous peoples had built thriving civilizations complete with megacities and advanced technology, and they had no intention of becoming slaves of Spain. But neither Columbus nor the explorers who would follow him, claiming lands in the names of distant kings and queens, would let these small complications bother them.

Because there was another concept that was even more powerful than *Finders Keepers*. And that was *Takers Keepers*.

In 1493, the pope, the leader of the Catholic Church, issued a decree called the "Doctrine of Discovery," which drew an imaginary line on the globe running from pole to pole about a hundred leagues west of the Cape Verde islands in the Atlantic Ocean. The decree stated that any land west of that line not already inhabited by Christians was Spain's for the taking.

That one letter written by one man set into motion all of Europe's claims on the Americas. It influenced the imperial ambitions of European nations all over the globe, including in Asia. And centuries later, the United States would use that same Doctrine of Discovery to justify pushing its borders west, seizing land from Indigenous Americans.

With the pope's decree, Spain was going to take all this "new land"—whether it was Asia or not—and they were going to keep it for themselves.

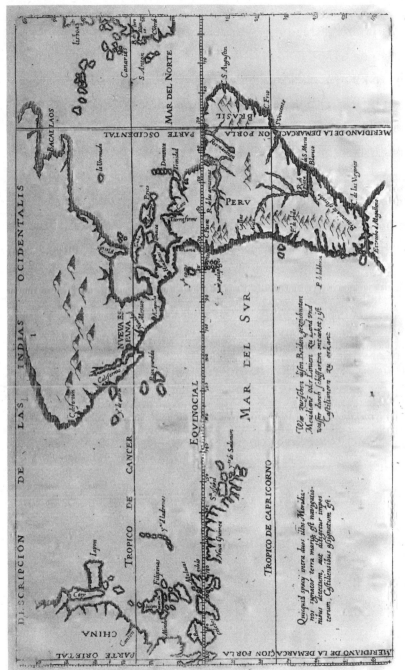

This world map from 1624 shows the line defined by the Doctrine of Discovery.

Christopher Columbus went to his grave believing wholeheartedly that his ships had landed in Asia. His blunder might be laughable if it weren't for the destruction and genocide that followed. His voyage ushered in the age of the Spanish Empire in the Americas. France and Britain would come along soon after. Millions of Indigenous peoples were killed by European settlers, either through direct violence or imported diseases. Communities were decimated, children were taken from their families, Indigenous people were removed from their homelands, and many were enslaved.

Columbus may have been mistaken about where he landed, but his voyage did connect Asia to the West in new ways. The Spanish Empire would eventually stretch around the globe, finally reaching across the Pacific Ocean to the shores of Asia (for real this time). When the first Asians arrived in the Americas, it was Spanish galleons that carried them there.

And some of those early ideas about Europeans being strong and superior and Asians being weak and inferior continued to shape how Asians were treated in the New World, and later, the United States.

FOLLOWING THE
ROUTES OF EMPIRE:
ASIANS IN "NEW SPAIN"

In the years after Columbus's journey, Spain applied *Takers Keepers* to huge swaths of North America, South America, and most of the Caribbean, an empire they called Nueva España, or New Spain. And then, in 1565, a Spanish monk named Andrés de Urdaneta charted a course from Acapulco, Mexico, all the way across the Pacific Ocean to a large group of islands off the coast of Southeast Asia. They would later be named in honor of King Philip of Spain: the Philippines. The Spanish Empire now spanned the globe.

Empires create routes, pathways that connect distant places to each other. Initially, the purpose of those routes is to transport physical goods from one end of the empire to the other. Once those routes are in place, people follow.

Throughout the age of the Spanish Empire, galleons (huge wooden ships described as "castles in the sea") departed the port city of Manila in the Philippines, their cavernous hulls loaded with Chinese porcelain, silks, and cotton. They carried emeralds, rubies, and diamonds from India, Cambodian ivory, Ceylon cinnamon, Sumatran pepper, and Persian carpets. All this treasure was bound for Mexico, where it would then travel across the Atlantic to Spain. On the return journey, the same ships carried chests full of silver pesos to pay for the bounty—the first international currency.

A sixteenth-century map shows the Spanish Empire in the Western Hemisphere. Unlike a kingdom, which is usually one region or territory that is ruled by a king or queen, an empire encompasses different territories and peoples that are sometimes all the way across the ocean from the government that reigns over them.

Filipino and Chinese sailors made up most of the crews on these ships (along with some Japanese, Southeast Asians, and South Asians). A long history of Asian maritime trade and exploration had made these men into skilled sailors. But on Spanish ships, they were treated little better than animals.

They were subjected to filthy conditions, given half the rations provided to the Spanish crew, and rarely paid the wages they were promised. Without proper clothing, some froze to death on deck during their journeys. With conditions that bad, is it any wonder that many sailors refused to make the return trip home?

When one Spanish galleon landed in Mexico in 1608, only five of the seventy-five-man Asian crew returned to the ship to make the journey back to Manila. The others stayed in "New Spain" to create new lives for themselves. These men—for it was almost entirely men who were recruited for such harsh working conditions—and many others who followed became some of the first Asian settlers in the Americas.

The Filipino fishing village of Saint Malo in Louisiana is believed to be the first Asian settlement in the United States, founded by sailors who deserted their ships in the 1840s. They represent the long line of Asians who had come as part of European colonization of the Americas.

After sailors, enslaved persons made up the next largest group of Asians coming across the Pacific to New Spain, where they became a part of the slave economies in the Americas.

Enslaved Africans had been brought to the Americas by the first conquistadors. And then for 400 years, more than 12 million enslaved people endured the passage from Africa across the Atlantic (up to one in five did not survive the crossing), to make European

RACISM

How does someone justify *Takers Keepers*? Not just the taking of land, but the taking and degrading of human life? How could anyone ever defend slavery or genocide? One of the ways has been to use racism. As historian Ibram X. Kendi explains, "A racist idea is any idea that suggests something is wrong or right, superior or inferior, better or worse about a racial group."

Dating back to the 1400s, European thinkers and rulers used racist ideas to justify *Takers Keepers* in Asia, Africa, and the Americas. They used them to justify the kidnapping and enslaving of Africans and sending them across oceans to live the rest of their lives in captivity. Africans were depicted as savage animals that needed taming. Asians were weak heathens who needed conquering. Indigenous peoples were uncivilized and did not deserve the lands that they possessed. All needed to worship the same god that the Europeans did. Racism powered colonialism, and vice versa. And when European settlers reached the lands that would eventually become the United States, racism came, too.

expansion and settlement of the Americas possible. Indigenous peoples were also enslaved in large numbers.

Although nowhere near as numerous as those enslaved from Africa, enslaved Asians also fulfilled the demand for labor. In the 1500s and 1600s, the city of Manila in the Philippines became a center of the slave trade. Portuguese enslavers captured people from Macao, India, Burma, Malacca, and Java for transport to

Racist justifications can look like this:

1. **Those people are inferior to us.** They look different from us. They act different from us. They don't believe in our religion. They are not as smart or civilized as us.

2. **Those people are dangerous.** They are hardwired to be violent. They will harm or dominate us unless we dominate them first, remove them, take away their rights, or destroy them. It's us or them.

3. **There are too many of them.** If we don't control them, they will multiply, and their numbers will overwhelm us.

4. **This is for their own good.** They are too uneducated and uncultured to know what's good for them. They don't follow our beliefs. By controlling them, we are saving them and helping them become better people: people like us.

Whenever we see or hear language like this, it should set off big alarm bells. Because too often, these words are followed by acts of cruelty, injustice, and violence.

Latin America and the Caribbean. Six thousand enslaved people from these countries entered New Spain every decade during the seventeenth century. Enslaved people from Asia were freed in 1672, and in 1700, a royal order prohibited the Asian slave trade. The transatlantic African slave trade, however, would continue its brutality for more than another century.

By the 1760s, Spain's age of empire was fading, and so too was its control over trade routes with Asia. The British Empire would soon rise up to become the world's leading *Taker and Keeper*, with the British East India Company exporting goods from Asia to ports all over the globe, and colonies in nearly every time zone of the world. In 1776, one of those British colonies decided to break off and do its own thing.

This new nation, the United States of America, would be founded on the highest ideals of humanity:

Justice.

Freedom.

Equality.

Like the British before them, and the Spanish before that, this brand-new nation would become more and more connected to Asia and Asian goods.

Eventually, Asian people followed as well.

BROKEN PROMISES:
AFONG MOY AND THE STRUGGLES
OF ASIAN LABORERS

In 1835, a Philadelphia newspaper advertised a traveling museum of Chinese "curiosities." For 50 cents, visitors could view furniture, paintings, vases, and an "unprecedented novelty": an Asian woman. Her name was Afong Moy.

1834 illustration of Afong Moy performing as "The Chinese Lady."

Just a teenager, Afong had been lured away from her family in China by American merchants who then brought her to the US to perform the role of an exotic item that would attract customers for their imported goods. Just like Europeans before them, Americans had become obsessed with things from the "Orient." It was seen as a status symbol to own Asian furniture and porcelain figurines and to drink Chinese tea. Chinese fabrics and silks became highly fashionable among the well-dressed set.

The merchants had promised Afong that she would be able to return to China after one year—a promise they likely never intended to keep. She was put on display for eight hours a day while spectators watched her eat with chopsticks and listened to her speak in Chinese. Thousands of people came to gawp at her (including then US vice president Martin Van Buren) in New York City, where she was first put on display. Her captors often highlighted her bound feet, even unwrapping them to show the bare skin to an entire auditorium of spectators. For a young Chinese woman at that time, it would have been a humiliating violation.

Afong protested, but what could she do? She was at the mercy of the merchants. For them, she was an object, like one of the teacups in their collection. But Afong was not a mere thing to be admired. She was a person—in fact, she was the first known Asian woman in the United States. And soon she would be followed by thousands of men, women, and children making their way to the Americas from Asia.

As soon as the United States became its own country, it made plans to trade with Asia. Just days after the defeated British left New York Harbor in 1783, American ships set off for China. Trading with China would bring wealth and security, something the new nation needed. By the time Afong Moy arrived in 1834, the United States was a prosperous young nation on the rise. Having broken free of the British Empire, America was now on its way to becoming an empire itself.

The US was building up its navy and expanding its territorial borders by wrenching land and power away from Native Americans. At the same time that Afong Moy was being displayed in New York City, Native Americans were being forcibly removed from their homelands in the Southeast and sent to so-called Indian Territory (present-day Oklahoma) under the Indian Removal Act signed by President Andrew Jackson in 1830.

As the United States grew older, the racist ideas that had justified *Taking and Keeping* grew with it. The nation that had been founded on ideals of freedom, justice, and equality continued to rely on land taken from Native Americans and the labor of enslaved Africans for a large portion of its economy.

The fertile land of the southern US, the Caribbean, and Latin America had proven to be a profitable machine, pumping out tobacco, rum, and sugar, and making vast amounts of money for the landowners and investors. For centuries, this machinery had been fueled by slavery.

The British Empire finally abolished slavery outright in 1833, and other European countries eventually followed. It took decades for the United States to join them. America fought a bloody civil war over the right to continue to enslave other human beings, and in 1865, it became one of the last "free" nations to free its slaves.

By the late 1800s, slavery had been abolished, but the economies that slavery had built were still humming along. There was *so much* money to be made. But who was going to do all that work and take the place of the formerly enslaved people? In the American South, free African Americans continued to be exploited for their labor: wrongly incarcerated and forced to work as "leased convicts," or caught up in a relentless cycle of "debt slavery" in which they toiled to repay bogus debts.

The British, whose empire included Jamaica, the Bahamas, and Guyana in a region of the Caribbean called the West Indies, turned to Asia and their other colonies to solve their labor problem.

Most of South Asia, including present-day India, Pakistan, parts of Myanmar, and Bangladesh, had been under British rule since 1858. They named this large region "British India."

The British colonizers immediately started to make changes to British India's economy and agriculture to benefit their empire. Local farming families suffered as they were forced to supply raw materials and cash crops to enrich Britain. This exploitation, combined with a population boom, caused people to leave their homes in droves.

Labor recruiters employed by West Indian plantation owners swept in to make offers that many could not refuse. *Did you just lose your farm? Do you owe money?* they asked farmers in the markets and railway stations where they hung out. There was work and easy money to be made abroad, the recruiters told them. All you need to do is sign this contract, work for a few years, make a lot of cash, and return home a rich man.

At least, that's what was *supposed* to happen.

Lured by these promises, more than 419,000 South Asians set off for plantations in the British West Indies as indentured laborers bound under contract known as "coolies." They were a diverse group: Muslim, Hindu, and Sikh, hailing from all over British India. Due to the physical nature of the farmwork, most were men.

And most found that their contracts were a complete sham.

Disease ran rampant in the filthy conditions. Workers slept in cabins that once held enslaved Africans. Their diet was poor. Their signing bonuses and wages were stolen from them. They were cruelly punished when they didn't meet expectations. The women who did sign on were paid less to do the same work as the men, and were even more vulnerable to abuse.

Some laborers didn't even come willingly: they were coerced or outright kidnapped. Just as racist ideas about the inferiority of Black people had justified slavery, so too did racist ideas about Asians justify the unequal conditions under which Asian indentured laborers worked and lived. Planters regarded them as "more akin to the monkey than to man."

Those people are inferior to us.

South Asians were purposely kept separate from Africans to prevent solidarity or coordinated uprisings. They rebelled anyway. Indentured laborers went on strike (refused to work). They marched and walked out on the job. The British government defended the system, but activists back in India were protesting. Finally, India's colonial government had had enough. By 1920, the indenture system was terminated. By that time, Britain had become a lion of the world, powerful and wealthy. And it had built that wealth on the backs of enslaved Africans and indentured South Asian laborers.

In the same way that British imperialism had caused suffering for South Asians, the growing presence of European powers in China and the unequal economic rules they put in place hurt Chinese farmers and workers. Even worse, China's southern provinces were battered by droughts, typhoons, rebellions, earthquakes, plagues, floods, and famines. Many started looking abroad for better fortunes and for sheer survival.

Beginning in 1874, some were sent to Cuba and Peru as indentured laborers. "I had to labor night and day," a man named Yang Wansheng recounted. "Suffered much from cold and hunger, was flogged when seriously ill, and was chained and imprisoned for resting a few moments." Conditions were so bad that many took their own lives.

And yet, like the South Asians in the British West Indies, the Chinese laborers found ways to fight back. Some went on strike or sabotaged their plantations. They filed protests in court, ran away, and in some extreme cases, they attacked their overseers. In 1877, Spain and China finally signed an agreement that freed all Chinese laborers in Cuba from their contracts.

Chinese laborers in South America were often treated cruelly by their overseers.

But even after gaining their freedom, the majority of Chinese indentured laborers didn't return home to Asia. Some had married and started families. Others were too ashamed to go back home without the wealth they had dreamed of. And others saw opportunities to work and make their fortunes in the Americas. Many stayed and created vibrant communities in Cuba. From there, some gradually began to make their way to the United States.

Over the centuries, enslavers, labor recruiters, steamship companies, and officials had built up a vast system to move enslaved and indentured people from Asia to Latin America and the Caribbean. As the world finally shifted away from the brutalities of slavery, that system also shifted, helping to bring the first free Asian immigrants to the United States.

As for Afong Moy, not much is known about her fate. Did she ever meet any of the other Asian immigrants who followed her arrival? Did she ever realize that although she was the first Asian woman in America, she would not be the last?

In 1835, Afong was brought to Washington, DC, to meet President Andrew Jackson—the first Chinese person to meet an American president. But she was eventually abandoned by the merchants who captured her. With no way to make money for herself, she ended up living in the care of a poor widow, in destitute conditions. Later, she joined P. T. Barnum's circus of human "curiosities," but soon after that, she disappears from written records.

Afong learned to speak English, but no one ever bothered to interview her about her treatment or experiences. We can only guess what she thought and felt. One thing is certain: she must have been very brave and very resilient to endure what she did, at such a young age, so very far from home.

Like the many Asian immigrants who would follow after her, she was a survivor.

WHAT'S IN A NAME?

When Afong Moy was brought to America, she was displayed alongside goods that were advertised as "Oriental": things like rugs, food, and ceramics. And even though Afong was not a *thing*, like a rug, she would have been called "Oriental," too. Why has this term been so popular, and what has it meant when it has been used to label Asian Americans?

When people like Marco Polo and Columbus set out to explore and conquer Asia in the name of the kings and queens they served, the "Orient" meant all of Asia, an array of lands and peoples that both fascinated and terrified Europeans. Even though Asia is a huge continent and there are many different peoples, religions, and nations, the word *Oriental* has come to mean "not from here." Exotic. Different. Inferior. Centuries later, Asian immigrants in the United States were labeled "Orientals," a code word for foreigners who were not as good as whites and who could never become Americans.

Another way Asian people have been singled out as "other" has been to call them "yellow," a reference to their skin color. Of course, the label is absurd (people of Asian descent have a wide spectrum of skin tones—none of them yellow), but racist labels are never about accuracy.

One of the first people to refer to Asians as yellow was the Swedish botanist Carl Linnaeus, who was separating humans into subgroups in 1735. He had already assigned white to Europeans, black to Africans, and red to Native Americans. What color should Asians be? Linnaeus decided to name them *luridus*, or pale yellow. These colors—white, black, red, and yellow—were used to separate populations into different races and place them on a scale in which white was at the top and Black was at the bottom. *Those people are inferior to us.*

OPPOSED TO JAP LABOR

Local Unions Ask for an Investigation of the Influx of Brown Men.

The arrival of hordes of Japanese laborers on the Sound, as announced in The Times, has resulted in action by the labor unions. At a meeting of the Western Central Labor Union held last evening a committee was appointed to make a complete investigation of the matter. President R. W. Moulton and Vice President Robert Pevler of the Union, who were appointed on the committee, were instructed to wait upon the immigration agents and ascertain what official action had been taken in the matter. The labor unions claim that both the contract and pauper labor sections of the immigration laws are being violated. The union officers stated last evening that if evidence of violation of the law could be secured prosecution would be commenced against the guilty parties.

This *Seattle Daily Times* article from 1900 illustrates that even major newspapers referred to Asian Americans using derogatory terms.

Soon, *yellow* did not only mean that Asians were inferior to whites. It also meant that they were a threat.

In 1895, Kaiser Wilhelm III, the ruler of Germany, awoke from a terrible nightmare. Supposedly, he had dreamed that the great nations of Europe were under attack by ruthless foreign invaders from the East. He immediately commissioned an art print of his vision and sent copies to several European leaders and to the US president. The print shows a group of warrior women representing the countries of Europe. The archangel Michael has come to them to warn of the foreign threat looming on the horizon. In the distance, Buddha rides a Chinese dragon (the "demon of destruction"), leaving burned cities in their wake.

The print was called *The Yellow Peril*, and it went viral, nineteenth-century style.

THE KAISER'S CARTOON.
"Nations of Europe! Join in the defence of your Faith and your Home!"

"Peoples of Europe, Guard Your Most Sacred Possessions" (1895) by Hermann Knackfuss.

It popularized growing fears of an Oriental invasion of the West (never mind that it was the Western empires that had invaded and taken possession of Asian lands). The concept of a yellow peril fit right in with white supremacist ideas swirling at the time that Asian countries threatened the security of the West, and that the future of the "white race" was under attack from the "yellow races."

Those people are dangerous.

In the 1960s, activists decided that they'd had enough of being called *yellow* and *Oriental*. It was time to claim a new name.

This new name would be about uniting Americans of Asian descent to push for a better world for all. In 1968, on the college campus of UC Berkeley, students formed the Asian American Political Alliance, one of the first Asian American organizing groups in the country. One of the AAPA's goals was to unite with other "Third World" people—including African Americans, Chicanos, Puerto Ricans, and Native Americans—to resist oppression and fight for equality.

It's taken decades of lobbying by Asian Americans, but now the term *Oriental* is finally on its way out. In 2009, New York governor David Paterson signed a bill that banned state documents from using the term *Oriental* when referring to people of Asian or Pacific heritage.

For as long as people of Asian descent have been in America, racists have used slurs to try to degrade them. It can be shocking to see that offensive terms such as *Mongoloids*, *Japs*, or *Chinks* were plastered across the headlines of newspaper articles well into the middle of the twentieth century, and even more hurtful to hear those slurs still used today.

By claiming a new name, Asian Americans rejected slurs and labels, and affirmed the right of every person to take pride in their identity.

IN SEARCH OF GOLD MOUNTAIN: MAMIE TAPE AND THE FIRST CHINESE IN AMERICA

In 1868, at the port of San Francisco, an eleven-year-old girl stepped off the steamship from Shanghai. She was all alone, with no parents. As a young girl traveling by herself, she would have stood out in the crowd of mostly male immigrants swirling around her on the docks.

The girl would later take an English name: Mary. On that day when young Mary stood on the crowded dock in San Francisco, she was just one face in the throng. But if anyone underestimated her then, they were mistaken.

In the mid-1800s, the United States of America was *Taking and Keeping* at an astonishing pace. The young country pushed its boundaries farther and farther westward, scooping up new territories through a war with Mexico and forcibly removing more Native Americans. And then, in 1848, a tiny nugget of gold was discovered in a riverbed in California. Just like that, the gold rush was on.

Once the news of the California Gold Rush reached China, it

spread like wildfire. Chinese farming families were still suffering the effects of European imperialism, internal divisions, natural disasters, and famine. Chinese immigrants boarded ships for "Gold Mountain," a name they used to describe the promised riches they believed awaited them in the US and Canada.

Very few Chinese actually struck gold in the fields. Instead, they began working in the mines, textile mills, cigar factories, and farms that had sprung up throughout California. And very quickly, they became indispensable to the state's economy.

Labor recruiters once again headed to China to search for workers. They were selling America hard: "Americans are very rich people," claimed one recruiter's advertisement. "They want the Chinaman to come. . . . Money is in great plenty and to spare in America." Unlike the indentured laborers who were taken to Latin America, these workers were not legally bound to others by a contract. But like those laborers, they were heavily recruited and often abused.

WORKING ON THE RAILROAD

In 1865, the first Chinese were hired by the Central Pacific Railroad to lay track for the great transcontinental railroad. This was the biggest transportation project America had ever undertaken. A rail system that could connect the entire country would be a technological feat that would change the fortune and future of the nation. But building it was a dangerous job. And the most dangerous, most dirty, least desirable parts of that job were left to the Chinese.

The Central Pacific and Union Pacific railroads were joined in Promontory, Utah, in 1869, completing the first transcontinental railroad line. Despite their large role in performing the labor, Chinese workers were left out of the official photograph documenting this historic moment.

Most Chinese workers in America found themselves doing the hardest jobs for the lowest pay. The Civil War had recently ended, and Asians lived an "in-between" existence among Black and white Americans. They had more freedom of movement and more privileges than African Americans, but they were not accepted as being equal to whites and were almost always paid less than white workers.

Rather than getting upset with the employers who paid unfair wages, white workers took their anger out on the Chinese for

While Irish immigrants worked to lay the eastern half of the rail-road, Chinese rail workers labored on the western half of the line, clearing trees, blasting rocks with explosives, shoveling debris, and laying tracks. The Chinese were both necessary (making up 80–90 percent of the work crews) and expendable to their employers. One newspaper estimated that at least 1,200 Chinese died building the railroad.

Central Pacific Railroad president Leland Stanford praised the Chinese workers and said that "without them it would be impossible to complete the western portion of this great National highway." How did he reward them? By paying them less and working them longer than their white counterparts.

The Chinese went on strike to protest. They refused to work unless they were paid fairly and treated better. The railroad bosses responded by cutting off their food supply. Isolated and starving, the Chinese were forced to give up.

When railroad work dried up, Chinese workers spread out. The demand for Asian labor was rising, and soon they could be found all over the country, from shoe factories in the Northeast to plantations in the South.

"stealing" their jobs. Sometimes, white gangs would roam through towns, beating up Chinese workers. This fear and resentment would continue to fester into something even more sinister and violent in the years to come.

Chinese immigrants often supported themselves by running small businesses, like laundries, restaurants, or stores. People at the time would stereotype them, saying that this was "traditional" Chinese work. But there was nothing especially "Chinese" about doing laundry or cooking food. They did this work out of necessity. Because they were shut out of other jobs due to racial discrimination, these were the only jobs they could get.

Working long hours in their businesses, often in isolation, immigrants found retreat and safety in the many Chinatowns that had sprung up across the country. New York's Chinatown hummed with activity and was also home to other immigrant communities: Irish, Italian, and Jewish. But the biggest and oldest Chinatown in America was—and still is—in San Francisco.

When eleven-year-old Mary stepped off her steamship and onto the docks of San Francisco, she was stepping into Dai Fou, or the "Big City," as the Chinese in America called it. It had boomed during the gold rush, and it was often the first port of entry for both immigrants and goods coming to the US from Asia. San Francisco was the place where Chinese immigrants could speak their native languages, visit with neighbors from back home, and get news about China. As one resident put it: "It is only in Chinatown that a Chinese immigrant has society, friends, and relatives who share his dreams and hopes, his hardships and adventures."

Once she arrived in San Francisco, Mary was taken in by the women who ran the Ladies' Protection and Relief Society, a home for "friendless or destitute" children. Mary learned to speak English and practice American customs, and became Christian. Like many other immigrants, she grew to revere the ideals of her new home: justice, freedom, equality.

When Mary was eighteen, she met a young Chinese milk delivery man named Joseph Tape. Joseph had also come to America

San Francisco Chinatown in the 1920s.

young: at just twelve years old. They likely bonded over their shared experiences of being outsiders in America and their dreams for the future. Joseph wanted to own his own business. Perhaps Mary talked of pursuing her musical and artistic hobbies. They spoke to each other in English, the only language they had in common since they had come from different parts of China and spoke different dialects. Six months later, the two were married. Over the years, they built a happy, successful life for themselves. They took road trips, bought a ranch, and by 1884, they had created a beautiful family with their four young children.

Mary lived a freer life than many Chinese American women at that time. Even though Chinatown bustled with activity, early female immigrants often felt trapped: oppressed by both racism and traditional expectations for women. And in the early days, when there were very few Asian women in the US, it could be very lonely for those who did arrive. But as more women began to immigrate and attitudes about women's roles changed both in China and the US, more women started to work outside their homes, educate themselves, and take part in community activities. They also became valiant champions for the rights of their children. Mary was one of these.

Chinese families in San Francisco's Golden Gate Park in the 1890s.

When her oldest daughter, Mamie, turned eight, Mary dressed her in a pretty outfit, tied a ribbon in her braid, and took her to enroll at the nearby Spring Valley Primary School. But before Mamie could take a single class, the school principal turned them away. Mary demanded to know why. She was well aware of anti-Chinese attitudes at the time, but her daughter was *American*. Mamie had been born in San Francisco, and she was just as deserving as any of the white children sitting in the school's classrooms. The Tapes lodged a complaint with the school board, but members only dug in their heels and passed a resolution that would prohibit all school principals from admitting any "Mongolian" child. If they did, they would be fired. Mary was furious.

She and Joseph sued the San Francisco School Board. Where was the justice? Where was the equality in denying her daughter an education? In a passionate letter, Mary shamed the board members for turning their backs on America's ideals:

I see that you are going to make all sorts of excuses to keep my child out of the Public Schools. . . . Is it a disgrace to be born Chinese? Didn't God make us all!!! What right have you to bar my child out of the school because she is [of Chinese descent]? There is no other worldly reason that you could keep her out.

The Tape family around 1884. Mamie stands in the center.

The Tapes' case went all the way to the San Francisco Superior Court. They and their lawyers argued that the decision to exclude Mamie from Spring Valley violated state school laws and the US Constitution. The school board disagreed and argued that existing codes allowed them to reject students who had "filthy or vicious habits, or children with contagious or infectious diseases." What they meant was that because Mamie was Chinese, she was automatically "filthy" and "diseased."

Those people are inferior to us.

In January 1885, Mamie Tape won her case. The court ruled that no child could be denied an education, and the public school system had to serve all students. It should have been a victory for the Tape family. But rather than admit Mamie, the San Francisco School Board rushed to create segregated schools to keep white children and Asian children apart. It would take another seventy years before the United States Supreme Court would declare that separate was *not* equal in *Brown v. Board of Education.*

Mamie Tape was never allowed to attend the school of her choice, but her family's fight for equality made a difference for many other students. Asian children now had a right to go to public school. And Mamie's case would lay the legal foundations to strike down later school segregation laws in California.

But there would still be a long way to go before Asians could partake in America's promises of freedom, justice, and equality. And anti-Asian racism in the country was about to reach new heights.

ONE THOUSAND QUESTIONS: TYRUS WONG, ANGEL ISLAND, AND CHINESE EXCLUSION

Would you be able to answer these questions?

What direction does your home face?
How many steps lead up to your front door?
Can you name all the neighbors on your street?
How many windows do your neighbors have?
What are the marriage and birth dates of all your family members?

These are just a few of the questions that nine-year-old Wong Gaing Yoo studied as he made the steamship journey from his birthplace of Guangzhou, China, to the port of San Francisco in 1919. A budding young artist, Gaing Yoo would have rather spent his time drawing, but his father instructed him to focus on studying the questions. Too much was at stake.

Immigrant inspection on board a ship docked at Angel Island in 1931.

As soon as their ship docked in San Francisco, Gaing Yoo and his father were taken to the immigration station on Angel Island in the middle of San Francisco Bay. Harsh-looking uniformed officials drilled them with these questions and tried to trick them into making a mistake. If the answers of father and son didn't match, Gaing Yoo could be sent back to China, alone.

In the years leading up to Gaing Yoo's journey, anti-Chinese racism and violence in the United States had swelled. The fascination that had caused Americans to greet Afong Moy as an exotic curiosity had twisted into hatred and resentment as more Chinese came to America seeking work.

At the same time, the US continued its violent wars with Native Americans, taking away more and more of their land, forcibly removing them, and exiling them to reservations. The US war with Mexico brought even more conquered territory and peoples into the nation. After the Civil War, slavery had ended, and African Americans were now counted as citizens during the Reconstruction Era. But the backlash was fierce. New laws passed by southern state governments limited the freedoms of African Americans, and anti-Black violence was widespread. While all these things were happening, Chinese immigrants started coming to the US and became the country's largest group of non-white immigrants. Where did they fit into America? Would they be welcomed? Or expelled?

On the one hand, the Chinese were a source of available labor that employers needed. But many others believed that the Chinese were a threat to American workers and to the United States itself. Politicians argued that white workers could not be expected to compete with the Chinese people's "machine-like" ways and their "muscles of iron." They were accused of being gamblers, gang members, and drug users.

Those people are dangerous.

Chinese immigrants were labeled as being dirty and bringing infectious disease to the United States. As early as 1876, San Francisco public health officials called the city's Chinatown "a plague spot" and a "laboratory of infection." Rather than blame public health problems on Chinatown's overcrowding or high poverty rate, the officials claimed that disease was a biological characteristic of being Chinese.

During the bubonic plague outbreak in San Francisco in 1900, city officials quarantined all 25,000 Chinese residents within the twelve-block neighborhood while white residents were allowed to move freely. And that same year, most of Honolulu's Chinatown was burned to the ground to destroy houses suspected of being infected with the plague.

In 1882, Senator John F. Miller of California argued that Chinese immigrants were a "degraded and inferior race." Other senators compared them to "rats," "beasts," and "swine." Like Native Americans and African Americans, they could never become American. They were a problem.

Those people are inferior to us.

There are too many of them.

And they must be stopped from entering the country.

Congress passed the Chinese Exclusion Act of 1882, the first immigration law that singled out an entire group based on their race. It forbade Chinese laborers from entering the United States. Six years later, the Scott Act denied entry to Chinese who left the US and tried to come back into the country. The Geary Act (1892) forced Chinese immigrants to register with the US government and required them to carry their identification documents with them at all times; they were the first immigrant group to be treated in this way.

The passage of these laws would spark some of the most violent and destructive racist campaigns in history.

By the 1870s, violence against Chinese was common throughout

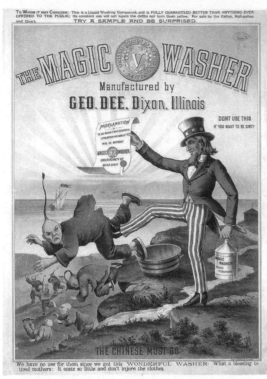

This 1886 advertisement for "The Magic Washer" laundry soap shows Uncle Sam kicking Chinese immigrants out of the United States and refers to the Chinese Exclusion Act with the tagline "The Chinese Must Go."

the American West. In 1871, nineteen Chinese were murdered in Los Angeles after a policeman was shot by a Chinese suspect. The police force did little as a mob of 500 people dragged Chinese people out of their homes, constructed gallows, and hanged them. It was one of the largest mass lynchings in US history.

The violence increased during the 1880s. In 1885, twenty-eight Chinese miners were killed in Rock Springs, Wyoming, and hundreds of other Chinese residents were driven out of town, into the desert. Later that year, a mob of 500 armed men forced all 800 to 900 Chinese residents in Tacoma, Washington, to leave the city, dragging some from their homes and pillaging their businesses. The next year, a mob of 1,500 forced all Chinese out of the city of Seattle.

Hatred was fierce on the West Coast, but the laws that targeted the Chinese were enacted on a national scale. The Chinese Exclusion Act was renewed by Congress in 1892 and 1902, and made permanent in 1904. In 1882, before the Chinese Exclusion Act went into effect, nearly 40,000 Chinese had entered the US. In 1887, only ten were admitted into the country.

The Chinese in America protested. They called out for change and hired lawyers to challenge the laws in court. When that didn't work, some found a way around them. Some tried to enter the US by crossing the border from Mexico or Canada. Others used false papers and identities. The first to be restricted, the Chinese became America's first "illegal immigrants."

The 1918 immigration application for Gaing Yoo, who later chose the name Tyrus Wong.

The Chinese Exclusion Act was designed to keep out the working classes, but it did allow certain types of people to enter the US from China: students, teachers, merchants, and diplomats and their families. If an immigrant could get papers that said they were from one of those groups, they might be able to slide in under the authorities' eye.

That's exactly what Gaing Yoo and his father were doing. He was one of thousands of "paper sons" who traveled to the US with false identity documents. In order to pass his immigration test, Gaing Yoo would have to pretend that his father was a merchant with a different name. Gaing Yoo had a different name of his own to memorize as well.

As his ship docked at the immigration station on Angel Island, Gaing Yoo must have been nervous. Everyone knew that it was difficult to get into the United States even if you were not using false papers. Unlike the immigrants arriving at Ellis Island in New York, those who came through Angel Island were not greeted by Lady Liberty's shining face or blazing torch. There was no poem inscribed to welcome the "huddled masses yearning to break free." Angel Island was a place of heartbreak.

Immediately after getting off the ship, Gaing Yoo and his father were separated. His father had been in America before, and so he was able to clear immigration quickly. But Gaing Yoo was taken to a wooden room crowded floor to ceiling with hundreds of steel bunk beds. Gaing Yoo was given a bed all the way up at the top, where it was hot and stuffy. Confused and afraid, the young boy cried. But there was nothing he could do but wait for his interview.

Days turned to weeks. He was the only child in the detention barracks. He didn't speak English. With no toys or books, no paper or paintbrush, the boredom was unbearable. Gaing Yoo was one of many children who would be separated from their parents for months or even years at Angel Island. "It was just like jail," he remembered.

Interrogation on Angel Island, 1923.

When immigrants arrived at Angel Island, they had to take off their clothes for physical examinations. Their bodies were inspected for "defects" and evidence of "Oriental disease." It was humiliating and traumatic.

Then came the interrogations. They were terrifying and universally dreaded. Most immigrants were asked hundreds of questions over the course of two or three days. Some were asked *one thousand* questions. If there was any mistake in your answers, you could wait weeks, sometimes months, for your case to be resolved. One Chinese immigrant named Kong Din Quong spent twenty-five months on Angel Island, only to be deported in the end. A few immigrants even tried to take their own lives. Poems carved into the wooden walls of the barracks reflect the despair and stress of those trapped in limbo:

There are tens of thousands of poems composed on these walls.
They are all cries of complaint and sadness.
The day I am rid of this prison and attain success,
I must remember that this chapter once existed.

43

Over a month after his arrival, Gaing Yoo was finally released into the arms of his tearful father. His experience on Angel Island would stay with him, but it did not break him. He enrolled in American schools and took on an Americanized version of his name: Tyrus Wong. Tyrus was finally able to access the paper and paintbrush he had dreamed of. He went on to graduate from art school, and then found a job at Walt Disney Studios as a low-level animator.

One day, Tyrus learned that Disney's team was having trouble creating the backgrounds for their new animated film, *Bambi*. He began painting landscapes using his own style, influenced by Chinese watercolor techniques. Walt Disney was bowled over when he saw them. No one else in the studio had ever painted like this. Tyrus was promoted and his landscapes anchored the *Bambi* film. In the movie's credits, he is listed only as a background artist. But his contributions made an impact on the entire studio, and his style would inspire a new generation of American animation artists.

Bambi was hailed as groundbreaking when it hit theaters in 1942—in large part because of Tyrus's art. One year after the film's release, the Chinese Exclusion Act was finally repealed. But the consequences of the law reverberated through Chinese American families for generations.

It also marked the fate of the many other Asian immigrants who came to America's shores. And even of Asian Americans born in the US.

WHO GETS TO BE AN AMERICAN?

Wong Kim Ark was born in San Francisco, California, in 1873. His parents were Chinese immigrants, and Wong had grown up in Chinatown and became a cook in one of the neighborhood's vibrant restaurants. When he was twenty-two, Wong took a trip to visit his parents, who had moved back to China. But when he tried to return to California, immigration officials would not let him reenter the US.

Even though Wong had been born in the United States, the officials argued that he was not a citizen because his parents were Chinese, and they were ineligible for citizenship under the country's naturalization laws and the Chinese exclusion laws. The officials kept him imprisoned on board the ship and ordered that he must be "returned" to China.

Wong Kim Ark

Be *returned*? How could a person be "returned" to a country they had never lived in? His whole life, he had only known America. He had been born on American soil. Wasn't that enough? Wong's situation placed him right in the middle of an ongoing debate over citizenship and what it meant to be "American."

As soon as the US had won its independence from Britain, the new nation had defined what it took to be an American citizen. In 1790, it was decided that only white, male property owners could "naturalize" (or become a citizen). Women, indentured servants, and any person of color were shut out.

After the Civil War, activists—including the African American writer and statesman Frederick Douglass—pushed for equal rights for newly freed slaves. In 1868, Congress passed the Fourteenth Amendment, which declared that any people born in the US, including former slaves, were citizens. This was called "birthright citizenship." In 1870, a new naturalization law allowed all persons of African descent, including those who had been formerly enslaved, to become naturalized citizens as well.

The citizenship question was resolved for African Americans. But what about others? Some argued that it didn't include Native Americans (it would not be until

After escaping slavery in 1838, Frederick Douglass became a national leader in the fight to abolish slavery. After the Civil War, Douglass advocated in favor of Chinese immigration.

1924 that Native Americans were granted full citizenship rights).

Others claimed that if you had Chinese parents (who by law could not become naturalized citizens), then you didn't qualify for birthright citizenship. Chinese Americans born in the US, one lawyer argued, were "utterly unfit" to be American citizens.

Which is exactly what officials said to Wong Kim Ark when he tried to reenter California. But this did not seem like equality, freedom, or justice to Wong. So he turned to the courts.

Wong's lawyer took his case to the Supreme Court and argued that, since Wong was a native-born citizen of the US, he was entitled to enter the country, and was not affected by the Chinese exclusion laws. They also argued that when Congress passed the Fourteenth Amendment, they meant to give birthright citizenship to *everyone*, regardless of their race.

Here is a beautiful thing, a truly great thing about this nation: any person, no matter where they stand on society's ladder, can take their case to the highest court in the land. Our courts are where anyone—even a restaurant cook, even a son of immigrants— can hold America's feet to the fire and say, "Hey, America, it's time to make good on those promises of freedom, equality, and justice."

Whether the courts make the decision to uphold those promises or not is another matter. Luckily, in the case of Wong Kim Ark, the Supreme Court decided that they would. Wong was granted his citizenship, and ever afterward, anyone who was born on American soil could call themselves an American citizen from birth.

When African Americans had fought for their right to be called

American citizens, they'd laid the groundwork for Wong to make his case. And in an age when the United States was excluding the Chinese, it was a Chinese American who also made America live up to its own principles.

UNWAVERING:
MARY PAIK LEE

Fourteen-year-old Mary Paik knew one thing for sure: she *would* go to high school.

It was a bold dream for a young Korean American girl living in California in 1914. For one thing, the books alone were an expense that few families could afford. Mary started saving early. She arrived at her middle school in Idria, California, early each morning to wipe the blackboards, sweep out the room, chop firewood for the stove, clean the outhouse, and ring the bell to call the students. For this, she was paid 25 cents per day.

Mary's family had immigrated to the United States from Korea in 1905 when she was five years old. Before they left, the extended Paik family had gathered together for a hard conversation. Japan had begun moving armed forces into Korea to seize control of the country. Japanese soldiers had taken over Grandmother Paik's house. Things were about to get very dangerous for Koreans in their own homeland. With heavy hearts, Mary's parents decided that their best chance for survival would be to leave their loved ones behind and sail for the United States.

The Paik family. Mary is the baby in the photo.

Like many Asian immigrants before them, the Paiks' first point of entry to the US was Hawai'i, where they joined thousands of Koreans who had been recruited to work in the islands' sugarcane plantations. At that time, other Asian workers were striking to protest harsh working conditions. The plantation owners realized that Koreans, in their desperate desire to flee starvation and oppression back home, could provide the missing labor that they needed.

But when Mary's family arrived in Hawai'i, they quickly learned that the recruiters' promises of opportunity were empty. They lived in a grass hut and slept on a dirt floor. Even though her father toiled

THE JAPANESE COLONIZATION OF KOREA

Korea's history is marked by centuries of fending off would-be colonizers: the European empires, the United States, China, and Japan. When the Japanese defeated Russia in the Russo-Japanese War in 1905, Japan showed the world that it was a formidable military power. The nation was poised to become an imperial force in Asia—one that could even rival the massive European empires that had gobbled up much of Asia. Japan seized the opportunity to finally acquire Korea and its resources for its own.

Over the next few years, Japan disbanded the Korean Army, shuttered newspapers, and closed local Christian churches and Buddhist temples. The Korean language was banned in schools, and Korean families were pressured to adopt Japanese names. In 1910, Japan annexed Korea as a colony outright. Protests by the Korean people were met with brutality, imprisonment, and execution by the new colonial government.

Koreans resisted Japanese oppression both within and from outside their country. They raised money, created nationalist organizations, and pressured the US government to stand up to Japan.

In the US, Korean Americans faced the same discrimination as Japanese and Chinese Americans had before them—lumped together with all "Orientals." But as people who were fleeing the colonization of their homeland, their heartache was unique. They were treated as outsiders in America, and they were also stateless. A Korean-language newspaper in San Francisco noted, "We have no country to return to. We are a conquered people." The fight for Korean independence became a defining factor of what it meant to be Korean American until Japan's defeat in World War II.

all day under the hot sun, they didn't have enough money left over to buy a single banana for their children to eat. As one Korean worker said, "Now that I look back, I thank goodness for the height [of the sugarcane stalks], for if I had seen how far the fields stretched, I would have fainted from knowing how much work was ahead."

In 1906, as soon as Mary's father could get them away from the plantation, the family sailed to California. It was just in time. In 1907, the US banned any Japanese from moving to the continental US from Hawai'i, and this rule applied to Koreans as well. Upon docking in California, the reception the Paiks received from the local people matched the cruelty of the laws intended to keep them out of the US altogether. At the pier, young white men taunted them and spat in their faces, and they kicked up Mary's mother's skirt. On the first day at her new school in Riverside, girls formed a circle around Mary and whacked her in the neck with their hands. Later, she learned that they were pretending to chop her head off.

"For Whites Only" signs were common all over the West Coast at that time. Just like African American and Latine people and Native Americans, Asian Americans were denied service in restaurants, barbershops, and swimming pools. They had to sit in a segregated section in movie theaters. They were harassed and violently attacked. And laws barred them from becoming naturalized citizens, too.

Mary once asked her father, "Why did we come to a place where we were not wanted?" Her father responded that "anything new and strange causes fear at first, so ridicule and violence result."

Two Korean American girls in Dinuba, California, 1919.

He said that their family must show white Americans that they were just as good as them by studying and working hard.

Mary's father's main concern was his family's survival. He knew that if he or his children spoke up every time they encountered racism, they would never rest. Worse, they could face violence. As the earlier massacres and mob attacks targeting Chinese immigrants had shown, it didn't take much to stoke white fear and rage against Asians. If the Paik family was going to survive, they would have to put their heads down and let their deeds prove their worth.

But Mary was not a grown-up with a family to protect. She was a child, and children are so good at knowing when things aren't fair. She bristled against the injustices her family faced.

How could Asians show their worth when the rules were so stacked against them?

In many California cities and towns, non-whites were not permitted to live in town with whites, and so the Japanese, Chinese, Mexican, and Korean families each had their own settlements on the city outskirts. The Paiks' first home was a one-room shack in a row of camp houses that had once been constructed to house Chinese railroad workers.

Mary's father did what most Korean immigrants did at that time: farmwork. Eighty-three percent of Koreans lived in the agriculture towns of California because farming was one of the only jobs open to them. This was difficult, "stoop back" work, as it was often called. Then, as now, it was hard to find workers who would do labor that was so harsh on their bodies. Farm owners recruited and often exploited minorities who had less ability to speak up for their rights or who had no other options. California law prevented Asian immigrants like Mary's father from owning land, so he had to be a tenant farmer, working land owned by someone else. If Mary's family wanted to eat, her parents had to take these migratory, seasonal jobs.

Now, at fourteen years old, Mary had graduated middle school, and her dream of going to high school was finally within reach. Her older brother, Meung, shared her goal of continuing their education and making a better life for themselves. Mary and Meung were good students, and their teacher informed them that they were the first Korean American children who had ever graduated from the middle school in that town.

But Meung's dream was not to be. Mary's father had taken a job in the local quicksilver mine, doing dangerous work that was steadily destroying his health. Their mother cooked, cleaned, looked after the young children, and worked in the fields when she could. Still, it was not enough to support the family. As a young man, Meung could get a job building roads. The pay from a job like that would be too much to give up just so he could go to school. On the day Meung realized this, Mary found him crying behind their shack. It was a bitter heartbreak, but there was nothing to be done.

Korean Americans stand with American and Korean flags in Dinuba, California, 1919.

When Mary's parents relocated to Willows, California, she went to the high school there. Her new teacher was a hateful man. When they came to the pages in their textbook about Chinese and Japanese history, he used horrible slurs when talking about Asians. And then he stared straight at Mary and said that "Korea was a wild, savage country" that had to be "civilized" by the Japanese colonizers.

Mary was furious.

True, her father had once told her that as Koreans, they must prove through their words and actions that they were just as good as white people. But he had also told her something that she had never forgotten: "Speak up when the occasion demands and stand up for what is right."

Mary waited until class was over and the other students left. She approached her teacher and said, "Where did you learn Asian history? You don't know a thing about the subject. If you ever say such things again, I am going to stand up in class and tell everybody in school where you go every Friday and Saturday night."

The teacher's face grew pale. "What are you talking about?"

Mary replied that because of racist laws, people of color were segregated into shabby neighborhoods where gambling and drugs were prevalent. Mary's family was forced to live there, but the teacher chose to visit those establishments. She knew because she had seen him with her own eyes.

After that, the teacher skipped past the pages about Asia without a word.

Throughout her life, Mary would never grow accustomed to the racism she experienced as an Asian American. She would recognize the common bonds between Korean Americans and other racial minorities in her community: Mexican Americans and African Americans. Mary would speak out against all forms of racial discrimination. She is one of the many Asian American heroes who are left out of the history books, but who have left their mark on our nation through their everyday acts of bravery.

STEADFAST SURVIVORS: THE BAGAI FAMILY

The arrival of Vaishno Das and Kala Bagai's family to San Francisco in 1915 was so unusual that it made the papers.

At the time, it was rare for South Asian families to immigrate to the United States. In fact, the *San Francisco Call and Post* reported that Kala was the "first Hindu woman" to enter San Francisco in a decade.

Like Wong Gaing Yoo and many thousands of other Asian immigrants, the Bagais' first stop was at Angel Island, where they were held for questioning. The interrogations came to an abrupt end when Vaishno showed the officials that he had brought money with him to start a new business: $25,000 in cash. Apparently, money answered a lot of questions.

Unlike Vaishno, most South Asian immigrants at the time arrived with little in their pockets. Many had been farmers back home, and they had come to work. While the British were bringing hundreds of thousands of indentured laborers from South

Asia to their colonies in the Caribbean and West Indies, other South Asians found themselves in high demand for jobs in the US.

By the 1910s, the US had fallen into a pattern with Asian immigrants:

Exclude the Chinese (after heavily recruiting them as workers).

Exclude the Japanese (after heavily recruiting them to replace the Chinese).

Exclude the Koreans (after heavily recruiting them, and also because at the time Korea was a colony of Japan, so exclude away).

The Bagai family in San Francisco. From left to right: Brij Bagai, Kala Bagai, Ram Bagai, Vaishno Das Bagai, Madan Bagai.

All this exclusion put US employers in a pickle. There was still *a lot* of work to be done. And the work was hard: jobs in the lumber, cannery, and agriculture industries of the American West were backbreaking and rough. They needed laborers. Preferably ones who could be underpaid.

American recruiters headed to South Asia.

In British India, the British colonial government had made a real mess of things for the "crown jewel" in their empire. Their policies had disrupted the economy, raised taxes, and displaced farming families. Vaishno Das Bagai was one of many who chafed under the restrictions and cruelties of British colonial rule while growing up in his hometown in Peshawar in present-day Pakistan. He became involved with groups that pushed for independence from Britain. After his parents died, he looked to the United States to pursue liberty and happiness. "I don't want to stay in this slave country," he said of his life. "I want to go to America where there is no slavery."

Labor recruiters took advantage of the dire situation and flooded the South Asian countryside with flyers advertising cheap fares on steamships bound for North America. Relatives and friends who had already immigrated to Canada or the US sent letters back home describing the wealth of opportunities to be had.

A diverse group of Sikhs, Muslims, and Hindus made their way to the US, with many coming from the Punjab region of present-day India and Pakistan, and from Bangladesh. Like scores of Asian immigrants before them, they arrived to find lives marked by hard work and discrimination. Farm owners paid them lower wages to toil under the brutal West Coast sun. South Asians often did the "roughest most unskilled work," and they were paid less than any other group.

Unlike Vaishno and Kala, most South Asian immigrants were young men who arrived alone. As they migrated from the West Coast to other American cities, some wanted to marry and settle down. But at the time, the US had strict laws that kept different races separate. It would not be until 1967 that laws banning interracial marriage were struck down across the nation. Where did South Asians fit into this racial system? For men with dark skin, African American communities were some of the only places they were accepted.

Interracial communities of South Asians and African Americans, Puerto Ricans, and West Indians formed in the American South and on the East Coast. In New Orleans, a number of Bengalis married and started families with African American women, and went on to play important roles in the history of Black New Orleans. In California, a vibrant Punjabi-Mexican community was established.

Similar to Korean Americans, most South Asian immigrants were united in their desire for independence for their home country. They did what they could to raise funds and raise their voices to free their homeland from British rule.

Vaishno Das Bagai in his store in San Francisco, 1923.

Vaishno Das Bagai loved his new life in the United States. He started a store in San Francisco called Bagai's Bazaar. Business was good. He wore crisp American suits and spoke fluent English with his customers. In 1921, he achieved a huge, proud milestone: he applied for and was granted US citizenship.

But even their wealth and success could not protect the Bagais from racism. When the family bought their first home in Berkeley, California, it seemed like their American dream was coming true. But when their moving truck pulled up to the house, they found that the neighbors had locked the doors to prevent them from moving in. Kala Bagai stood in front of the truck, loaded with all their furniture and belongings, and told her husband, "I don't want to live in this neighborhood. I don't want to live in this house, because they might hurt my children, and I don't want it."

Vaishno agreed. The family climbed back into the moving truck and they drove back to San Francisco to live above their store.

In the early 1900s, anti-Asian racism was strong and growing. First, the Chinese were said to be an immigrant threat and unfit to become naturalized citizens. Then Japanese and Koreans were targeted. In 1905, a mass meeting was held in San Francisco to launch the Japanese and Korean Exclusion League to advocate for a "white man's country" and to lobby for the exclusion of Asian immigrants. When South Asians started to arrive in the US, the organization changed its name to the Asiatic Exclusion League so that it could better push for the exclusion of South Asians as well.

These racists claimed there was a "Hindu problem" threatening the US (even though South Asians were a diverse group of Hindus, Sikhs, Muslims, and other faiths). Religious Sikh men who wore the *dastar*, a turban head covering important to their faith, were particularly targeted. In 1911, the US Immigration Commission reported that South Asians were "universally regarded as the least desirable race of immigrants thus far admitted to the United States," and recommended that the US should figure out a way to prevent them from coming into the country.

White workers charged that South Asians were going to "steal" their jobs, just as other Asian workers had done before them. Violence broke out in 1907 in Bellingham, Washington, when 1,000 union mill workers marched down the main streets, shouting, "Drive out the Hindus." A mob of white men pulled South Asians out of their homes and dragged them off streetcars. By nightfall, 200 South Asians had been taken to jail, and the next morning the rest of the community had left town, with the taunts of the crowd ringing in their ears.

Newspapers referred to the "Hindu Invasion" and the "Tide of Turbans" taking over the West Coast. Lawmakers argued for excluding South Asians, just like they had excluded the Chinese.

In 1917, Congress passed a new immigration act that set up an "Asiatic Barred Zone." The law shut out immigrants from most of the Middle East, and East and Southeast Asia. It also included all of present-day India and Pakistan. Since the Chinese and Japanese had already been excluded by other laws and diplomatic agreements, it was clear that the law was meant to target South Asians.

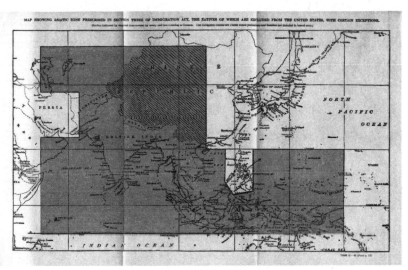

Map of the Asiatic Barred Zone.

Like Wong Kim Ark, Mary Tape, and others before them, South Asians also took their fight for equality to the courts. Bhagat Singh Thind was a Sikh man who had come to the United States as a student. When World War I broke out, he enlisted in the US Army and was promoted to the rank of sergeant. After the war, Thind was allowed to become a naturalized citizen. But shortly afterward, US officials changed their minds.

In 1923, Thind took his case to the US Supreme Court. He argued that he was descended from the Aryans of India, and so belonged to the Caucasian race (along with other white people). During a time when American laws and public opinion were stacked against people of color, claiming to be white was Thind's only option to access the same rights as white people had.

But the Supreme Court rejected this idea. The court went on to say that everyone knew that when the law said "white," that meant white *and* European. Everyone else was shut out from becoming an American. Thind was stripped of his citizenship.

Bhagat Singh Thind, 1918.

Soon, other South Asians were affected. Including Vaishno Das Bagai. The US government argued that Vaishno was not white and that he had illegally become a naturalized citizen. It revoked his US citizenship.

Without citizenship, Vaishno was no longer eligible to vote or own land. He was forced to sell his home and his store in San Francisco. When he tried to return to Peshawar to visit his family, the US refused to grant him a passport so that he could travel. They suggested that he apply for a British passport.

This was a slap in the face. Vaishno had already renounced his British citizenship as a protest for Indian independence. He would never go back on that.

In despair, Vaishno took his own life in 1928. He left a heartbreaking letter that was published in the newspaper:

> Now what am I? What have I made of myself and my children? We cannot exercise our rights. . . . Humility and insults, who is responsible for all this? Me and the American government. . . . Obstacles this way, blockades that way, and the bridges burnt behind.

Vaishno left behind Kala, his widow, and three young sons. His death was a heartbreaking tragedy, but it was not the end of the Bagai family's story in America.

Kala would pick up the pieces of her life, and—like so many immigrants who had come before her—she would go on.

AN ALL-AMERICAN GIRL: MONICA ITOI SONE

Six-year-old Monica Itoi was spitting mad.

It was 1925, and her parents had just informed her that she had to go to Japanese school. But Monica already went to elementary school every day. She walked there each morning from the hotel her parents owned and lived in, skipping through the streets of her Seattle neighborhood with her best friend, Matsuko. And now she was supposed to go straight from school to *more* classes?

At Japanese school, students learned to speak and write in Japanese. They were taught correct posture and to practice the proper manners of good Japanese children. Monica didn't want to take classical Japanese dance—she wanted to be a ballerina and twirl around the stage in a pink tutu. What was the point of learning all this Japanese stuff, anyway?

Monica was *American*.

Monica Itoi Sone at Hanover College, 1943.

After the Chinese, Japanese immigrants were the second-largest group of Asians to come to the US. For over 200 years, Japan had almost entirely isolated itself from trade and travel with Western nations. When Japan finally lifted those restrictions in 1854, American traders and labor recruiters poured into the country, desperate for workers to toil in Hawai'i's sugar plantations. Japan also encouraged its citizens to emigrate. There had been a population boom, and the Japanese government hoped that by sending poor farmers and workers abroad, they might prosper and send money back home to their families.

Workers loading sugarcane on carts, Hawai'i, ca. 1917. Initially brought to the islands to perform hard labor, Asian immigrants struggled against an oppressive plantation system that often pitted them against each other and against Native Hawaiians. But while Asian Americans suffered from the racism of the plantation system, they also participated in the settler system that continues to oppress Native Hawaiians.

After World War II, Asian Americans built wealth and political power, making gains that often came at the expense of Native Hawaiians, who are still more likely to experience homelessness, poverty, and health issues than other ethnic groups in the islands. Some Native Hawaiian groups continue to press for independence, land reclamation, and a return of sovereign rights to the Hawaiian people.

As more Japanese made their way from Hawai'i to settle in other parts of the US, they took the jobs that were available. In Seattle, Monica's father worked on the railroad, cooked on ships that sailed back and forth to Alaska, and—like many Japanese—pulled vegetables in the fields as a farm laborer. Japanese community leaders started looking for ways to buy and own the farms. But first they had to overcome barriers put in their way.

In response to growing anti-Japanese racism, California had passed the Alien Land Law of 1913 to bar Japanese immigrants (or "aliens ineligible for citizenship") from owning or leasing land. This was not only a form of economic discrimination; it was an organized attempt to drive Japanese immigrants out. But Japanese Americans got around these laws by teaming up with other families to purchase farms, and by putting the land in the names of their American-born children. They also challenged the laws in court, with mixed results. Despite their struggles, many Japanese American farms thrived. By the eve of World War II, Japanese Americans grew 95 percent of California's snap beans and peas, 67 percent of the state's tomatoes, and 44 percent of its onions.

Japanese Americans also built tight-knit communities to help them survive in the US and to keep their heritage alive. Many had their own schools to teach their nisei (American-born) children Japanese language and customs. Like Monica, most nisei children lived in two different worlds. At home or in Japanese school, they spoke Japanese, practiced polite manners, and learned to be dutiful to their parents. But they also spoke fluent English at public school, listened to hip new American records, played baseball, and learned the latest dance steps.

Their issei (Japan-born) parents also felt conflicted. On the one hand, they maintained ties to Japan and took pride in their heritage, and they wanted their children to do the same. On the other hand, they were proud of their American sons and daughters and of the lives they had built in the US. And they thought that their children's lives might be easier the more they could *assimilate*, or become more like the white children around them. So even though Monica's issei parents made her go to Japanese school, they also encouraged her to be a good, all-American girl.

Japanese American Boy Scouts, Seattle, 1935.

In reality, trying to assimilate did little to protect Japanese Americans. Anti-Japanese racism grew out of the earlier anti-Chinese movement. Japanese Americans were threatened, harassed, and attacked with little interference from the police. In 1907, anti-Japanese race riots took place up and down the Pacific Coast, from San Francisco all the way up to Vancouver, Canada, where a mob wielding stones and clubs destroyed almost every business owned by Chinese or Japanese people. The hatred fed on itself. Acts of public violence encouraged America's political leaders to create even stricter immigration laws. And in turn, the racist language used by politicians fanned the flames of the mob.

For years, anti-immigrant leaders in the United States had pushed for laws that shut out Asians and other immigrants. In 1907, US president Theodore Roosevelt was in a delicate position. States like California were pressing him to keep out the Japanese. But the president did not want to offend the government of Japan, now a strong and mighty empire that wanted to be seen as an equal among the other empires of the world. So the two nations worked out a deal. The US would not just exclude Japanese immigrants as it had the Chinese with the Chinese Exclusion Act. Instead, it would negotiate a "gentlemen's agreement" that allowed the Japanese already living in the US to reenter the country if they left and to bring their families over from Japan. In exchange, Japan would not send any new workers to the US.

But this was not good enough for the racist anti-Japanese leaders and their followers. Japanese immigrant women were coming over and having US-citizen children. The Japanese American population was growing. And they were staying.

The anti-Japanese movement was part of growing anti-immigrant sentiment and hatred, or *xenophobia*, that was gripping the entire country in the early twentieth century.

In the 1920s, lawmakers decided to close America's gates to immigrants. In 1921, the US Congress passed an immigration law that set up quotas, or limits, for the amount of people who could immigrate from each country. But some thought this law didn't go far enough.

XENOPHOBIA

Throughout our history, Americans have been taught to be afraid of many things, including and especially immigrants. This fear is called *xenophobia*, and it comes from two Greek words: *xenos* (foreigner or stranger) and *phobia* (fear). Xenophobia is a fear that's so great that we are supposed to do whatever is necessary to protect ourselves from dangerous outsiders. It's about "us" versus "them." And it's more than just prejudice or bigotry. In the US, it's been built into our laws, politics, and our definition of who counts as "American."

From the very beginning of our country's founding, white supremacists in America labeled Native Americans and African Americans as "others" and as "outsiders" and have discriminated against them. How we have treated Native Americans and African Americans has influenced how we have treated immigrants.

Xenophobia is a form of racism. This is how it works: It labels certain immigrant groups as the "good" ones, the nonthreatening kind who contribute to America. Then there are the "bad" immigrants. The ones who don't speak English, don't assimilate, are dangerous and unfit to be citizens. America has welcomed and even recruited "good" immigrants while we have banned and expelled the "bad" ones.

Who is considered "good" versus "bad" has been a matter of national origin, religion, class, gender, and sexual orientation. But especially race.

For much of our history, immigrants and refugees from Asia, Latin America, and Africa have been considered "bad" immigrants. They have been blamed and scapegoated for taking away jobs, bringing crime and disease into the country, changing America from good to bad. And the US has banned, restricted, and deported them.

So in 1924, Congress passed a new immigration law that allowed even fewer people from central, southern, and eastern Europe to come to the US and denied entry to anyone who was "ineligible for citizenship." As the Supreme Court had stated in the Bhagat Singh Thind case, to become a naturalized citizen, you had to be white and European.

Because almost everyone else in Asia had already been excluded through other laws, the target of this 1924 law was the Japanese. It worked. The door to immigrants from Japan (and from all other parts of Asia) was now closed completely.

Like other Asians before them, the Japanese insisted that America's ideals of equality and justice should apply to them, too. In 1922, businessman Takao Ozawa challenged the US's restrictions on citizenship in the Supreme Court. Takao had immigrated to the US as a student in 1894. He spoke fluent English, was a Christian, and worked for an American company. In other words, he had tried his best to assimilate and to be a "good" American. Knowing that only whites were given the full range of rights in America, Takao also argued that although he was Japanese, his skin was "white in color"—even paler than some immigrants from Europe. It was similar to the argument that Bhagat Singh Thind would make one year later. "In name, I am not an American," said Ozawa. "But at heart I am a true American."

Takao's plea was denied. The Supreme Court ruled that the country's existing naturalization laws specifically stated that only white people could become naturalized citizens. It didn't matter how much you assimilated. It didn't matter how well you followed the rules or how "American" you tried to be. Unless you were white—meaning white *and* of European descent—in America, you were unfit to become a real American citizen.

On a beautiful summer day in 1937, Monica Itoi piled into a car with her friends and drove out to a swimming pool in the countryside. When they arrived, the pool manager blocked their entry. "Sorry," he said stonily. "We don't want any Japs around here."

The kids replied, "We're not 'Japs.' We're American citizens." They got back into the car and drove away, but the humiliation stung.

Monica had felt this sting before. Newspapers were full of grotesque cartoons of Japanese people: bucktoothed, beady-eyed, with huge glasses and bowed legs. Across the ocean, the nation of Japan was becoming a *Taker and Keeper* of its own, expanding its army and imperial ambitions, first by seizing Korea and then by fighting in China. Whenever stories of the Japanese Army advancing into China made the news, Monica could feel people glaring at her in the streets. Now Japan, not China, stood as the dominant military power in Asia. Western powers feared that Japan would attempt to conquer the West next. The threat of Japan (the country) and Japanese Americans (the human beings) started to merge into one.

For a long time, all Asians in America had been lumped into one big group of "Orientals." But now people started to make distinctions between the Chinese and the Japanese. China was labeled as being a "backward" civilization that was beset with problems.

Those people are inferior to us.

Japan, on the other hand, had modern industries and a powerful military. The Japanese were not labeled as a weaker, inferior race, as other Asians were. In fact, that's what made them so threatening: they were not inferior to whites. Instead they were portrayed as cunning, sly, heartless. A peril.

Those people are dangerous.

As Monica Itoi grew older and finished high school, her future should have been bright and wide open. Her parents had promised to send her to university, and she and her friends spent their days dreaming of college football games and which classes they would take. But that summer, Monica's father delivered crushing news: she wouldn't be going to university after all. Instead, her parents would send her to business school, so she could learn skills that would land her a steady job.

Monica wept over her broken future. But she also knew that her father was right. This was no time for lofty college daydreams. Something was in the air.

People had started to whisper of war. And the whispers were growing louder.

THE YELLOW PERIL

How the Japanese Crowd Out the White Race.

THERE will doubtless be opposition to the exclusion of the Japanese. A little of it will come from emotional people, on what they imagine to be ethical grounds, but in the main the opponents of the movement will be those who are perfectly confident of their own ability to sustain themselves under any competition, and desire to employ gang labor. Except in household service the Japanese are not yet displacing white labor in cities to any great extent, except as they work upon their own account, as small merchants, cobblers, gardeners and similar occupations. In starting these independent occupations of their own they are far more alert and aggressive than the Chinese. And when they enter an industry the white men have to leave it. An Alameda correspondent says that the Japanese have taken possession of the shoe repairing business in that city to the exclusion of white men. The white shoemaker, as a rule, has a family and a home. The Japanese, as a rule, has neither. Freed from those expenses he can and does do work at prices which get the trade, and the white man is driven out. The market gardening industry has to some extent been occupied by Chinese, but in the main it has been held by white men, mostly Europeans, accustomed to spade culture, but having in them the making of good American citizens. In some places this is rapidly passing to the Japanese, because their living expenses are nominal. With no idle mouths to feed they herd in old shacks, and can exist and lay up money where any white man will starve.

What is already happening in a few places will happen everywhere if the invasion is not stopped. If it be true that the Japanese have driven the white shoe repairers out of Alameda, for example, can any one suggest what will prevent them from driving the white men out of that and similar occupations in every other city in America? Like causes produce like results. It is only a question of numbers, and the numbers are only a question of time. By acting now, while the numbers are still small, we can act calmly, discussing the subject with the Japanese Government in the most friendly spirit, with the view to the best interests of both races. By waiting until a great part of the mischief has been done we simply invite the passion, the rioting, and the bloodshed which is absolutely certain to follow, and a settlement of the question in the midst of international excitement and friction. One already hears of this Japanese invasion in all parts of the State—from Vacaville, Fresno, Visalia, the Sierra fruit districts—everywhere. The settlements are not general. A spot here and a spot there is occupied as conditions happen to favor. They are getting possession of the gang labor generally—on the railroads, in the beet fields and in the large orchard holdings. If it is not stopped there will be serious trouble, just as there would be trouble in Japan if Americans were invading Japan as Japanese are invading America. The only question is whether our authorities will act as the result of such quiet and passionless discussion as the "Chronicle" is conducting, or insist upon waiting until actual race warfare compels action.

Newspapers like this one in San Francisco spread the idea that Japanese immigrants had been sent from Japan as an advance colonizing force. Books and pamphlets described how a Japanese invasion of the West Coast would happen, assisted by the Japanese who were already living there, the "enemy within our gates."

ALREADY AMERICAN: FRANCISCO CARIÑO

In the 1930s, the world simmered just below its boiling point.

The United States was in the midst of the Great Depression. Almost one-quarter of the country's workforce couldn't find a job, and farmers were having to foreclose on their farms and homes. In the Southern states, African American activists fought back against the Jim Crow laws that enforced segregation and their unequal treatment. In Germany, Adolf Hitler had named himself the Führer and was hard at work making good on his promises to exterminate the Jewish people and claim Europe for the "pure" white race. In Asia, Japan expanded its empire by invading the Chinese region of Manchuria.

And along America's West Coast, racist laws were working to exclude another community: Filipinos.

But unlike the immigrants from China, Japan, Korea, or South Asia, there was an issue with shutting out Filipinos. They were, technically, already Americans.

In 1898, the United States had fought and won one of the shortest wars in its history: the Spanish-American War. By the end of this four-month war, the US had acquired Puerto Rico, Guam, and the Philippines, and was given temporary control of Cuba.

Filipinos resented being handed over from one colonial ruler to another. They wanted full independence. American leaders claimed to respect this, but they also decreed that the Philippines was "not ready" to be independent: the people were too backward, too "uncivilized" and "savage," to take care of themselves. At best, they were referred to as children in need of guidance. President William Howard Taft called the Filipino people America's "little brown brothers." The US just *had to* be their colonizers.

This is for their own good.

The Filipino people fought for their independence for three years, but in the end—after 4,500 US soldiers were killed, and over 1 million Filipino civilians died from battle, disease, and starvation—the US military prevailed. The Philippines became a territory of the United States, with promises that one day—when it was "ready"—it would gain its independence.

With the Philippines in its possession, the United States became a transoceanic empire, a *Keeper* on a global scale.

Born in the Philippine town of Candon in 1900, Francisco Cariño grew up viewing himself as both a Filipino and an American. By the time he was a little boy, American missionaries, teachers, doctors, and colonial officials had come to work in the United States' new colony. Like many Filipino children at that time, Francisco attended American-style schools, where he learned US geography, history, and government. His teachers spoke of America's founding ideals: freedom, equality, justice. They taught Francisco that the US was "a land of the brave and the free, land of opportunity," and he pictured it as "a land of Paradise."

Filipinos were given the status of US nationals, but they were not given citizenship. This meant that they did not have the rights of US citizens, such as the right to vote. But, unlike other Asians at the time, they could come to the United States with few restrictions.

Filipino workers, 1928.

They were also the only foreign nationals who were allowed to enlist in the US armed forces. They were only allowed to join the US Navy, and most were given "women's work": they became navy stewards who cooked and cleaned for the officers. Still, military service had benefits and good salaries. Thousands of Filipinos enlisted.

Like so many Asians before them, they were heavily recruited by US employers desperate for workers (now that they had already excluded the Chinese, the Japanese, the Koreans, and the South Asians). After being taught about the best of America, many Filipinos were open to these pitches to migrate to the US.

Like so many Asians before them, Filipinos often headed to the Hawaiian Islands first, and then continued east to the work awaiting them on America's West Coast. And like so, so many Asians who had come before, they were met with disappointment.

For Filipinos like Francisco Cariño, who had grown up believing that they were a part of the American story, the heartbreak was especially sharp.

When he moved to Los Angeles in his twenties to continue his college studies, Francisco was horrified to learn what most Americans believed Filipinos were actually like. He saw museum exhibits that portrayed them as savages who used primitive tools. Books about the Philippines showed pictures of nude people and claimed that all Filipinos lived the same lifestyle. Even missionaries who had been to the Philippines played up stories of the "dark side" of the culture.

He also faced racism. When Francisco tried to get a haircut, the barber shouted at him, "Are you a Jap?" Landlords would not rent to him. When he tried to find summer work, Francisco

Filipino lettuce field laborer, 1939.

was turned down at employment agencies because he was Asian. When he applied for a restaurant job, the manager turned him away, saying, "I'm sorry—you are dark." In California towns, signs proclaimed "Positively No Filipinos Allowed" or "No Filipinos or Dogs."

Because of this racism, even highly educated Filipinos found themselves stuck with low-paying jobs: dishwasher, waiter, janitor. In California, most Filipinos—around 60 percent—worked in "factories in the fields"—agriculture.

By the 1920s and 1930s, California agriculture was a booming multimillion-dollar business with a long history of exploiting immigrant workers. Chinese, Japanese, South Asians, and Koreans had made up the first wave of farmworkers. Now Filipinos and Mexicans made up much of the workforce. They migrated with the shifting harvests. "When asparagus is over here, we are already done, getting ready for grapes," said one migrant worker. "Then the grapes [are] over, the tomatoes are ready to ripen up. We had to go where the job was. Name it, baby, I was there. . . . I just wanted to work."

In Salinas, Filipinos worked eight to ten hours a day for 15 cents an hour. Dust from the fields coated their lungs and covered their skin. Though Filipinos protested their working conditions, like many immigrants before them, they were the ones who were blamed for taking work away from whites and for keeping wages low.

White migrant workers were moving into California as part of the great Dust Bowl migration from Texas, Oklahoma, and Arkansas. They came from regions of the country where Jim Crow segregation, the Ku Klux Klan, and lynchings were common. Xenophobia, racism, and economic anxiety all combined to fuel violence. It happened first in Watsonville, California.

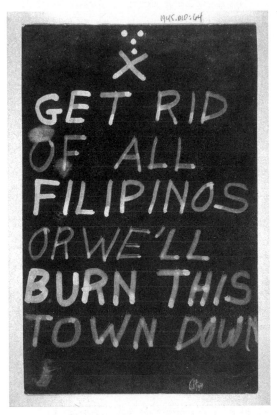

Letter threatening Filipino Americans from around 1929–1934.

In 1929, a Watsonville newspaper published a photo of a Filipino man and a white girl embracing. The couple was engaged and they had the blessing of the girl's family, but the sight of a man with brown skin touching a white woman sent people into a rage. A mob of 400 white men attacked a Filipino dance hall, leading to four days of rioting. Many Filipinos were beaten, and one was killed. In 1933, California passed a law making it illegal for whites and Filipinos to marry.

Political leaders began to call for the exclusion of all Filipinos. They circulated bills and drafted legislation. But Filipino American leaders pointed out that if they passed such laws, the United States would be the only imperial power in the world to ban its own people from entering another part of its empire. If the US wanted to keep Filipinos out, they would have to grant the Philippines its independence first. Wouldn't you know it? The politicians backed down.

Filipino Americans built up strong communities to protect and support themselves. "Little Manilas" sprang up in Los Angeles, Seattle, Chicago, and Washington, DC. The biggest Filipino American community was in Stockton, California. There, returning migrant farmworkers could rest and recuperate. They could pick up the latest newspaper from the Philippines and grab a plate of adobo from a local café. They could dress in their nicest clothes and go out with friends to dance to the latest songs played by local jazz bands.

Filipino Americans also turned to their communities to organize for their rights. The first Filipino farmworkers' strike took place in Watsonville, California, in 1930. They refused to work until their

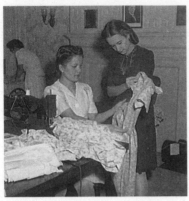

Filipino Women's Club of Washington, DC, in the 1930s.

employers met their demands for better wages, working conditions, or both.

Filipino laborers formed unions and elected leaders to speak for them and do the negotiating with employers and growers. In 1933, 700 lettuce workers walked off the job to protest their low 20-cents-an-hour wage. But ultimately, the strike failed because the growers brought in other Asian and Mexican American laborers to work the harvest. This strategy of using one racial group against another so that no one could earn higher wages or better working conditions was something the growers did repeatedly.

The next year, the Filipino Labor Union tried again. This time, the strike was made up of 6,000 Filipino lettuce pickers and white laborers who packed and stored the lettuce. The strike brought the lettuce industry in Monterey County to a standstill. The growers called in local police and armed vigilantes to beat up the workers. The union headquarters were raided, and the union leaders were arrested. And yet, the Filipino workers stood their ground and were able to negotiate to get double their wages.

The lettuce strike put Filipino labor organizers on the map and introduced them to other labor organizations in America. The Filipino agricultural unions grew stronger, larger, and more confident over the years, becoming an essential part of the movement for the fair and just treatment of all American workers.

Despite the discrimination he faced in the United States, Francisco Cariño continued to see the best of America and believe in the basic goodness of humanity. "People have no biological differences," he told an interviewer. "If we come to think (I hope it would soon come) that we are of *one* race, then the relations of all peoples in all ways must be so intimate and so strong as to bind them in one golden cord of love." Francisco believed that Americans could live up to their potential, and he hoped for a changing of their hearts.

He would eventually get his wish. Some racist attitudes did change, and Filipino Americans were more accepted in the US. But change came in an unexpected way, and after great turmoil.

The world, which had been on simmer, was about to erupt into a full, roiling boil.

MILITARY NECESSITY: THE INCARCERATION OF JAPANESE AMERICANS

Daniel Inouye was a high school student in Honolulu, getting ready for church on the morning of December 7, 1941. He was tying his necktie, listening to the radio, when suddenly the music stopped. The disc jockey screamed, "Pearl Harbor has been bombed! . . . The Japanese are bombing Pearl Harbor!"

Daniel and his father rushed out to the street and looked toward the US naval base at Pearl Harbor, where black puffs of smoke rose into the sky. Suddenly, three fighter planes screamed overhead. They were bombers that had just made their run over the harbor. The planes were gray, with red circles painted on the sides—Japanese planes. In that moment, Daniel felt that life as he knew it was over. "Because obviously the pilot in that plane looked like me."

The attack on Pearl Harbor was the nightmare that many Japanese Americans had been anxiously anticipating for years. Monica

Itoi's parents, who had decided not to send her to college, had been right to fear the distant rumblings of war. Japanese Americans were worried that they would bear the blame for any aggression by Japan against the United States.

They were right.

The bombing of Pearl Harbor took place in the morning. By that evening, the FBI was bursting into Japanese American homes, tearing the siding off the walls and flipping over the furniture, looking for "evidence" that would implicate the owners in spying for Japan. Monica Itoi's family hurried to destroy anything in their home that would give the impression they were sympathetic to the Japanese. They burned Japanese-language books, magazines, and wall scrolls. Precious dolls and toys from their childhood were tossed into the furnace.

The FBI continued to comb through the community, arresting leaders and labeling them as "enemy aliens." Within forty-eight hours, 1,291 Japanese had been arrested. The response was so swift because the US government had been preparing for it.

The year before, the US had passed an Alien Registration Act, which required all "resident aliens" (noncitizens) over fourteen years old to register with the government and have their fingerprints taken. The FBI had been collecting information on Japanese communities and had created lists of individuals they suspected of being spies or informants for Japan. The list included anyone who'd had contact with the Japanese government—no matter how harmless it was. Even Japanese-language teachers and Buddhist monks were automatically put on the list.

Japan had indeed placed spies in the US in its embassies. And during World War II, nineteen Americans were arrested for serving as agents of Japan. All of them were white.

The vast majority of Japanese Americans were overwhelmingly loyal to the United States. Even the US government reports said so. Agents who had been sent by President Franklin D. Roosevelt to secretly investigate Japanese communities on the West Coast reported that first-generation immigrants would eagerly become US citizens if they were allowed to do so. And the US-born nisei were "eager to show their loyalty" to America.

It didn't matter.

Within days of the attack, the US secretary of the navy toured the wreckage of Pearl Harbor and told reporters that it had been "the most effective fifth column work of the entire war." A *fifth column* is a military term for a group of people who work from within one nation to undermine it. In other words, he was making the accusation that the Japanese people of Hawai'i had betrayed their own country to help Japan kill their fellow Americans.

Those people are dangerous.

President Roosevelt appointed General John DeWitt to be in charge of defending the entire West Coast of the US. DeWitt believed the Japanese in the US were a huge threat to national security. "The Japanese race is an enemy race," he stated. "It makes no difference whether he is an American citizen, he is still a Japanese." He put it more bluntly for reporters: "A Jap is a Jap."

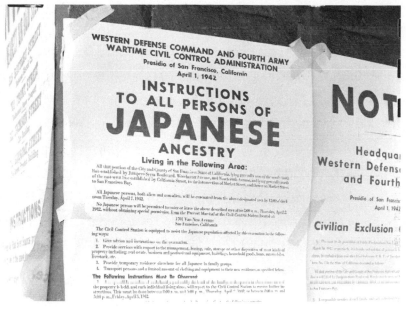

San Francisco posting of Executive Order 9066, ordering the forced removal of Japanese Americans.

DeWitt saw plots everywhere, and he believed even the most outlandish conspiracy theories about Japanese Americans, like that they were sending Japan messages with flashlights or that Japanese farmers were pointing the caps on their tomato plants toward air bases. "The very fact no sabotage has taken place to date is a disturbing and confirming indication that such action *will* be taken." The absurd logic is enough to make your head spin.

It certainly didn't make sense to the US-born nisei, like Monica Itoi and her classmates. Why would they betray America? They *were* Americans. The accusation was disgusting and offensive.

Akiko Kurose was fifteen years old at the time, and she couldn't believe that her loyalty might be questioned. When her father told her that he was worried that their family could be in danger when the US went to war with Japan, she thought, "Why should that bother me? You know, I'm an American." But the harsh reality quickly rose up. The next day at school, her teacher confronted her and said, "You people bombed Pearl Harbor." She was shocked. "All of a sudden my Japaneseness became very aware to me. I no longer felt I'm an equal American."

The racist hysteria grew as bad news trickled in from the Pacific. The more ground the Allied forces lost, the more the public clamored to deal with the "threat" of Japanese Americans. Newspaper editorials like this one from the *Seattle Times* cried out for action: "Herd 'em up, pack 'em off. . . . Let 'em be pinched, hurt, hungry and dead up against it." The author conceded that, sure, maybe most of the California Japanese were loyal, but "if making one million innocent Japanese uncomfortable would prevent one scheming Japanese from costing the life of one American boy, then let the million innocents suffer."

Those people are dangerous.

It's us or them.

Politicians who were running for office were especially vocal about imprisoning Japanese. They knew that by shouting loudly for Japanese removal, they could paint a picture of themselves as pro-American, which would be great for capturing votes.

In the White House, there was a battle raging over what to do about the Japanese in America. Officials in the War Department pushed for mass removal and incarceration. On the other side, lawyers for the Justice Department worried that arresting American citizens based

Waiting for the Signal From Home . . .

Honorable 5th Column

WASHINGTON
OREGON
CALIFORNIA

TNT

Dr. Seuss

One of several cartoons with racist depictions of Japanese that Theodor Geisel (who wrote children's books under the name Dr. Seuss) drew during World War II.

on their race would punch a huge hole in the Constitution.

The pressure was on from politicians, the press, and military advisers. In the end, the decision rested with President Roosevelt. FBI and Naval Intelligence reports said that the Japanese in America posed no threat to national security. Even so, on February 19, 1942, the president signed the executive order to remove and imprison Japanese Americans in twenty concentration camps set up in remote areas all over the US.

It was called an "evacuation."

Japanese Americans were given one week to get ready.

One week to sell your house, your business, your belongings.

One week to figure out what to do about all the thousand details of your life.

Seven days to say goodbye to your only home, not knowing if you would ever return.

Monica Itoi's family packed necessities in their suitcases—only what they could carry with two hands—and made their way to their assigned assembly point. As they boarded their bus, newspaper photographers rushed into the crowd. They called out to a bewildered young couple and their son and told them to turn and smile for the camera.

Members of the Mochida family awaiting their forced removal in Hayward, California, in May 1942. Like all other Japanese Americans, they were forced to wear identification tags during what the government called "evacuation."

This is for their own good.

They were rounded up with no evidence, no trial, no proof of wrongdoing. Anyone with one-sixteenth or more Japanese ancestry was targeted as a prisoner without trial. Why? It was a "military necessity," the US government claimed.

And yet, in Hawai'i, the site of the bombing of Pearl Harbor, where there were many more Japanese Americans living, there was no mass removal. Japanese American residents made up a huge percentage of the workers in agriculture, transportation, and carpentry. Taking them away would have damaged the economy. And so only 1,504 Japanese in Hawai'i were taken into custody and incarcerated in camps on the mainland. The rest of the Hawaiian Japanese were placed under severe restrictions for the duration of the war. The difference in the treatment of Japanese Americans in Hawai'i and on the mainland should have raised red flags about whether the mass removals were indeed "necessary."

During the "evacuation," Japanese farmers who had barely scraped through the Great Depression and were just starting to get on their feet again had to abandon their fields just before the harvest. Buyers took advantage of the chaos and offered insultingly low prices to Japanese Americans who were forced to sell their homes and businesses. It was the first of many bitter pills to come.

Altogether, 120,000 Japanese Americans, including those transferred from Hawai'i, were removed from communities up and down the West Coast and incarcerated in military camps. Almost 6,000 babies were born behind barbed wire. The camps were in remote and inhospitable places in the "heart" of America: barren

Topaz, Utah; arid Poston, Arizona; the swampland of Jerome, Arkansas; and blisteringly hot Manzanar, California.

Minidoka Relocation Center, Hunt, Idaho, August 1943.

When Monica's family arrived at their desolate camp at Minidoka, Idaho, they felt "as if we were standing in a gigantic sand-mixing machine. Sand filled our mouths and nostrils and stung our faces and hands like a thousand darting needles."

There was an equal sting—one of betrayal. Even the youngest "evacuees" could see that their rights had been trampled by the country they had pledged allegiance to every morning in school. Thirteen-year-old Tom Akashi couldn't understand why all the Japanese had to leave their homes. He thought, "Where's my rights? What's happening to me?"

For the Japanese Americans filing into the makeshift camps, the same questions swirled inside their heads.

What is happening?

And when—if ever—will it end?

AMERICA'S CONCENTRATION CAMPS

Once President Roosevelt's executive order went into effect, Japanese Americans were rounded up and sent to "assembly centers" to wait for shipment to incarceration camps. Some of these places were hastily converted stables or racetracks that still stank of the animals that had lived in them. Families had to make their own mattresses out of bags and straw.

After waiting for weeks or months in these filthy centers, Japanese Americans were sent to one of ten War Relocation Authority camps scattered in some of the most desolate and remote areas of the country. The camps have commonly been called "internment camps," but "internment" would only technically be correct if the prisoners were nationals of another country that the US was at war with. The places where Japanese American citizens were sent were, by definition, concentration camps: large numbers of inmates were forced into crowded housing with inadequate living conditions, where they had no legal hearings or any recourse to challenge their imprisonment. The terms *incarceration*, *confinement*, and *removal* more accurately describe Japanese Americans' experiences in the camps, rather than *internment*.

The camps were surrounded by armed guard towers and barbed

wire. Entire families would have to share a small one-room barrack with a single light bulb overhead.

The food was bland and loathsome, and the surroundings were bleak. Prisoners who were housed in the desert camps, like Minidoka, Idaho, where Monica Itoi and her family were sent, endured triple-digit heat in the summers, frigid winters, and unrelenting sandstorms. When it rained, crossing from the barracks to the communal bathroom or dining hall meant slogging through ankle-deep mud. For months, they didn't even have flush toilets, but had to use a pit in the ground until proper facilities were finally built.

Japanese Americans did what they could to retain their dignity and provide as much stability for their families as possible. Prisoners helped to set up schools within the camps. They started sports teams and held exercise classes. Some families started gardens to supplement their poor diets. But the conditions of the camps took their toll on families, and the degrading treatment was especially hard on the older issei.

Japanese Americans board a bus bound for the camp in Manzanar, California, 1942.

The barracks of the Jerome Relocation Center in Denson, Arkansas, 1942.

An inmate in his barrack room at the camp in Manzanar.

Accomplished artist Chiura Obata leads an art class for students at the Tanforan camp.

A crowded general store at the Tule Lake Relocation Center in Newell, California, 1942.

"GOOD" ASIANS, "BAD" ASIANS

An interesting thing happened to Asian Americans once the US entered World War II.

Until this point, Asians had been lumped into one giant faceless group of "Orientals" who were unfit to be citizens and needed to be banned from the US. But now America was at war with Japan. China, Korea, and British India were US allies. American soldiers were fighting alongside Filipino soldiers in the Philippines. Suddenly, Americans were told they needed to stop seeing all Asians as threats to America and unlearn the habit of treating them all the same. Instead, they needed to learn to tell the "good" ones from the "bad" ones. And who was "good" and who was "bad" depended on who the US was friends with and who it was at war with.

In the 1930s, sympathy for Chinese Americans had been building as Japan rose as a threat in the Pacific, eventually going to war with China. Then, when Japan bombed Pearl Harbor, China became an important member of the Allied forces in the war.

This man is your FRIEND

Chinese

He fights for FREEDOM

★ ★ ★

Poster created by US Office of Facts and Figures, 1942.

Twelve to fifteen thousand Chinese Americans signed up for US military service—20 percent of the adult male Chinese population. Others built ships and worked in factories. Chinese American women also went to work in shipyards, hospitals, and for the Red Cross. All these things caught the attention of the media, which highlighted the patriotism of the Chinese. Sometimes, the turnaround in attitudes was so swift, it was a wonder people didn't get whiplash. One congressman said, "All at once we discovered the saintly qualities of the Chinese people. If it had not been for December seventh, I do not know if we would have ever found out how good they were." New Yorker Harold Lui recalled, "All of a sudden, we became part of an American Dream."

In 1943, President Roosevelt signed the Chinese Exclusion Repeal Act, ending more than sixty years of Chinese exclusion. "China is our ally," President Roosevelt said. "Today, we fight at her side." With this new law, Chinese immigration still remained very low. But Chinese immigrants were finally allowed to become naturalized American citizens.

Attitudes about Filipinos changed quickly, too.

President Roosevelt had famously called the Japanese attack of Pearl Harbor on December 7, 1941, a "day that will live in infamy." But the next day brought even more destruction, and it's a day that is often left out of World War II histories.

The United States was a transoceanic empire in 1941. The Japanese military knew it had to hamper the US's ability to counterattack, and so they set out to hobble every US military outpost in the Pacific. That meant bombings of the islands of Guam and Midway, and Wake Island. And it meant a full invasion of the Philippines.

In 1943, China's first lady, Soong Mei-Ling, or Madame Chiang Kai-shek, toured the US in an effort to increase support for China in its war against Japan. She visited President Franklin D. Roosevelt and First Lady Eleanor Roosevelt at the White House. On February 18, 1943, she became the first Chinese person and only the second woman to address a joint session of the US Congress. Her speech was a resounding success and changed many Americans' views on China.

On December 8, 1941, Japanese planes departed their bases at Taiwan and headed for Luzon, the largest island of the Philippines and the site of a large US and Philippines military presence. Soaring just out of reach of American antiaircraft weapons, the Japanese dropped streams of bombs on Luzon's airfields, wiping out communications and destroying planes that had been left sitting on the ground. In a repeat of the surprise attack on Pearl Harbor, the American air force in the Philippines was nearly flattened by a lack of planning, improper equipment, and poor decision-making.

Poster created by Philippines Office of Special Services, 1943.

Stories trickled across the Pacific into the United States about the brave Filipino soldiers fighting side by side with American soldiers. The battles and shared suffering in the Philippines came to symbolize interracial brotherhood. These stories transformed opinions about Filipinos from backward "little brown brothers" to loyal allies who shared a common goal of freedom and democracy with the US. US First Lady Eleanor Roosevelt said that the fighting on the Bataan peninsula in the Philippines was "an excellent example of what happens when two races respect each other."

When Carlos Romulo, a former military aide to General Douglas MacArthur and brigadier general in the United States Army, toured the United States in 1944, he visited Stockton, California, where there had previously been a violent attack on the Filipino American community. He urged white Americans to set aside their racism against Filipinos: "Take them into your hearts as the seventeen million Filipinos took into their hearts the seven thousand American soldiers who fought for you, for us, for freedom in Bataan. Don't discriminate against them, please. Smile at them when you meet them in your street."

For Filipino Americans, the Japanese invasion was a direct attack on their homeland. Thousands rushed to military recruiting offices with love for both the Philippines and the US in their hearts. But only those born in the United States (and who were thus citizens) were allowed to join. Even as US nationals, Filipinos in America were ineligible to enlist in the armed forces. They protested until President Roosevelt changed the draft law. On the same day that the president signed the executive order for the removal and incarceration of Japanese Americans, Filipino Americans were recruited into segregated infantry units of the US Army. Over the course of the war, more than 7,000 Filipinos served in these regiments, or contributed in other ways. Some were even sent behind enemy lines to destroy Japanese communications or provide intelligence.

Like Chinese Americans, Filipino Americans found new opportunities opening up for them. Stockton, already home to the biggest Filipino community in the US, became a huge center of shipbuilding and weapons factories. Because so many American men were off fighting in the war, employers needed anyone who was able to work, even minorities who had been previously turned away. Many Filipino Americans shifted from working in the fields to working in better-paying factory jobs. Farmworkers, household staff, and restaurant workers became welders, technicians, and assembly line workers.

California changed its land laws to allow Filipino Americans to lease land, and they were encouraged to take over properties that had been held by the Japanese Americans who were being imprisoned in camps. In 1946, the US passed the Luce-Celler Act, which finally allowed both Filipinos and South Asians to become naturalized citizens.

The change in public attitudes was dramatic, but as Filipino American writer Manuel Buaken observed, "We Filipinos are the same—it is Americans that have changed in their recognition of us."

For Korean Americans, World War II did not bring such swift changes as it did for Chinese and Filipino Americans. For one thing, the US government still officially classified Koreans as subjects of Japan. It didn't matter that Koreans in America had been pushing for their country's independence from Japan for decades.

On the day of the Pearl Harbor bombing, Mary Paik stopped in at her local grocery store. She was now grown up and farmed fifty acres of land in South Whittier, California, with her husband and young children. When she walked in the door, a group of people stared at her with hatred. One man said, "There's one of them . . . Japs now." The store owner stuck up for her, saying, "Shame on you, all of you. You have known Mrs. Lee for years. You know she's not Japanese, and even if she were, she is not to blame for what happened at Pearl Harbor!"

Mary had left her one-year-old son in the truck outside, and when she came out, she found three teenagers with their fists raised, ready to strike him. She was appalled. "Does it take three of you to beat up a one-year-old baby?"

Korean Americans enlisted in the service, hoping that an Allied victory against Japan would finally mean independence for Korea. They saw it as a patriotic duty, both for the United States and also for their ancestral homeland.

Some of this Asian American patriotism had an ugly anti-Japanese side. Some Korean American leaders spread false rumors about a Japanese fifth column in the Pearl Harbor attack and called for the forced removal of Japanese from the West Coast. They were far from alone. Most American newspapers and magazines were doing the same.

Asian Americans, particularly those who lived on the West Coast, feared that they would be mistaken for Japanese. Mary Paik Lee and her family were afraid to go out at night. "Many [Koreans] were beaten during the day," she recalled. "Their cars were wrecked, their tires were slashed. . . . Many just assumed that all Orientals were Japanese. . . . It was a bad time for all of us." Korean and Chinese Americans started wearing buttons on their clothes that said "I am Chinese" or "I am Korean" so that they wouldn't be mistaken for a Japanese American.

Susan Ahn Cuddy had grown up hearing about her father's fight against Japanese imperialism in Korea. When World War II began, she became the first Asian American woman to enlist in the US Navy and soon became the navy's first female gunnery officer. She was so good at her job that she eventually became a combat air tactics instructor. Like many Asian American women in the armed forces, Ahn faced both sexism and suspicion. But no one could deny her skills. "It was funny because she was tiny," her son later recalled. "So she would have to really contort herself to pull back on the firing mechanisms to load the machine gun."

Chinese   *Japanese*

HOW TO TELL YOUR FRIENDS FROM THE JAPS

Of these four faces of young men (*above*) and middle-aged men (*below*) the two on the left are Chinese, the two on the right Japanese. There is no infallible way of telling them apart, because the same racial strains are mixed in both. Even an anthropologist, with calipers and plenty of time to measure heads, noses, shoulders, hips, is sometimes stumped. A few rules of thumb—not always reliable:

▶ Some Chinese are tall (average: 5 ft. 5 in.). Virtually all Japanese are short (average: 5 ft. 2½ in.).

▶ Japanese are likely to be stockier and broader-hipped than short Chinese.

▶ Japanese—except for wrestlers—are seldom fat; they often dry up and grow lean as they age. The Chinese often put on weight, particularly if they are prosperous (in China, with its frequent famines, being fat is esteemed as a sign of being a solid citizen).

▶ Chinese, not as hairy as Japanese, seldom grow an impressive mustache.

▶ Most Chinese avoid horn-rimmed spectacles.

▶ Although both have the typical epicanthic fold of the upper eyelid (which makes them look almond-eyed), Japanese eyes are usually set closer together.

▶ Those who know them best often rely on facial expression to tell them apart: the Chinese expression is likely to be more placid, kindly, open; the Japanese more positive, dogmatic, arrogant.

In Washington, last week, Correspondent Joseph Chiang made things much easier by pinning on his lapel a large badge reading "Chinese Reporter—NOT Japanese—Please."

▶ Some aristocratic Japanese have thin, aquiline noses, narrow faces and, except for their eyes, look like Caucasians.

▶ Japanese are hesitant, nervous in conversation, laugh loudly at the wrong time.

▶ Japanese walk stiffly erect, hard-heeled. Chinese, more relaxed, have an easy gait, sometimes shuffle.

A few weeks after the bombing of Pearl Harbor, *Time* and *Life* magazines ran racist stories that drew connections between a person's physical appearance and their status as an ally or enemy of the US. Stories like these helped to spread the idea that all peoples of Japanese descent were enemies to the US.

While the status of other Asian Americans rose during World War II, life was on hold for the incarcerated Japanese Americans. Months of bleak conditions in the camps became years. The daily routine was degrading and dreary, and the lack of basic items like nutritious food and adequate clothing was taking a toll. Some of the worst treatment occurred at the largest camp in Tule Lake, California, where any Japanese Americans who were labeled as being "disloyal" or "problems" were sent. Prisoners were beaten, and workers were tear-gassed when they tried to protest their working conditions. For months, the inmates were subjected to curfews and searches by armed guards.

Families tried their best to make their stark barracks more comfortable. Monica Itoi's father built cabinets and furniture from scrap lumber. Children went to a makeshift camp school, taught by those who had been teachers in their former lives. A small library was started with books donated from nearby towns. And when moments of joy pierced the dreariness, families embraced them.

One day, Monica's brother, Henry, surprised his family with an announcement: he had proposed to his girlfriend. They were going to be married—right away. Monica, her mother, and the new bride rushed around in a flurry of preparations. They secured a one-day pass into town to buy a wedding dress, while Henry went to the courthouse for a marriage license. After the wedding, the entire camp gathered for a reception for the new couple in a bare recreation barracks.

The make-do ceremony and celebrations had been brief, and just in time.

Henry had just volunteered to serve in the US Army.

LOYALTY

Their own government had barged into their homes without reason. They and their loved ones had been forced to leave everything behind and live for years in concentration camps. And then one day, officials came to the incarcerated Japanese Americans and asked them to prove their loyalty to the United States.

In early 1942, War Relocation Authority officials entered the camps and gave Japanese Americans a mandatory questionnaire that was designed to test each person for "Americanness vs. Japaneseness." Two of the questions were particularly upsetting. Question 28 asked:

Would you be willing to swear unqualified allegiance to the United States of America . . . and forswear any form of allegiance or obedience to the Japanese emperor, or any foreign government, power or organization?

For most, even asking this question was an insult. They had never pledged their allegiance to Japanese emperor Hirohito in the first place. Hadn't they repeated over and over that they were loyal to America?

The question also made them afraid. There was little information provided to the people in the camps. Everything was so confusing—including why they were even in the camps in the first place. Some people whispered rumors that all people of Japanese ancestry would be shipped to Japan. If they chose to denounce ties to Japan, would they be left stateless—without a passport and belonging to no country? Then what would happen to their rights?

Question 27 was posed to all men eligible for the draft (a law that required all males of a certain age to serve in the US military).

Are you willing to serve in the armed forces of the United States on combat duty, wherever ordered?

When Monica and her friends read this question, they fumed at the audacity. The US had ignored its very ideals when it forcibly removed and incarcerated Japanese Americans. And now it wanted them to fight in the war to defend those ideals? And what would happen if they were sent to Japan? Would they be forced to fight against men who might be their own relatives?

Ten to fifteen percent of Japanese Americans answered "no" and "no" to these two questions, and many did so out of protest of their treatment. The "no-no's," as they were called, were automatically considered disloyal to the US and were transferred to the

Tule Lake camp, a maximum-security facility where dissent from inmates was answered with violence by the authorities.

But many other young Japanese men, like Monica's brother, Henry, answered yes to both questions. If they had been outside the camp, they would have signed up to serve in the military without hesitation. But when recruiters showed up to the camps and told them they would be serving in segregated units, the men balked. They didn't want to be segregated from other Americans anymore. They should be treated like any other soldiers.

The recruiters told them that this was a chance to change people's minds and to show the whole country how Japanese Americans were loyal to the US.

They shouldn't have had to prove anything. It was so unfair. But many agreed that this would put the question of their loyalty to rest, once and for all. And then there was this: What choice did they have?

More than 33,000 Japanese Americans served in the US military during World War II. Some served in engineering battalions that constructed defense projects in Hawai'i. Those with Japanese-language skills served in the secretive Military Intelligence Service, where they translated enemy correspondence and interrogated POWs. President Harry Truman later called them the "human secret weapon for the US Armed Forces."

Nearly 500 Japanese American women served in the military as clerks, typists, cooks, and drivers, which freed up men to fill much-needed combat roles. Some women became translators in the Women's Army Corps, and those with nursing experience served in the Army Nurse Corps and Cadet Nurse Corps.

And 18,000 Japanese American men served in combat, most of them in the 100th Infantry Battalion and the legendary 442nd Regimental Combat Team. Together with the 100th Infantry Battalion, the 442nd is the most decorated unit in US military history for its size and length of service.

Most members of the 442nd were nisei from Hawai'i—including Daniel Inouye, whose family church visit had been interrupted by the attack on Pearl Harbor.

Daniel was second lieutenant of his platoon in April of 1945, when he led his soldiers in an assault on a German-held ridge in San Terenzo, Italy. As Daniel's platoon attacked, German machine guns opened fire on them. Daniel was hit, but he called to his men to keep advancing, throwing grenades as he crawled toward the machine gunners.

Daniel pulled the pin on his grenade and reached back to throw it into the gunners' nest. A German soldier jumped up in front of Daniel. "One instant he was standing waist-high in the bunker, and the next he was aiming a rifle grenade at my face from a range of ten yards. And even as I cocked my arm to throw, he fired and his rifle grenade smashed into my right elbow and exploded. I looked at my dangling arm and saw my grenade still clenched in a fist that suddenly didn't belong to me anymore."

The grenade was still live, and seconds away from exploding. Daniel used his other arm to wrench the explosive from his destroyed hand and lobbed it at the Germans. Even then, Daniel didn't stop, firing his gun with his one uninjured arm until he was shot in the leg and lost consciousness.

Daniel Inouye (far left) and other wounded US soldiers, including future fellow US senator Robert Dole (next to Inouye), recover at a US Army hospital in Michigan, 1946–1947.

The 442nd is also famous for its rescue of the "Lost Battalion," 200 soldiers who were cut off from the rest of their unit and under heavy German fire in the Vosges mountains of France in the winter of 1944.

After two previous rescues had failed, the 442nd—who were already exhausted from ten brutal days of fighting to liberate French cities—were ordered to attempt a rescue of the Lost Battalion. The motto of the 442nd was "Go For Broke," and that was what they did.

Wounded Japanese American soldiers of the 100th Infantry Battalion, 34th Division, returning to the United States, 1944.

After fighting the Germans for five days with little progress, the nisei soldiers had no choice but to go straight up the ridge in a "banzai charge." "The fighting was really fierce," recalled Fred Matsumura. "We were fighting, in the forest, you know. And they're throwing shells at us; every time the shell hit the tree, it burst like geysers." Finally, they reached the Lost Battalion and were able to get them to safety.

But the heavy losses to their own unit were devastating. Dozens of trucks had carried nisei soldiers to the battlefield. After it was over, the survivors fit in the back of a single truck.

As the war neared its end in 1945, nisei soldiers also liberated

Jewish prisoners from the Dachau slave labor camps. They found the camps mostly empty because the Nazi guards had already begun marching away from the advancing Allied armies, forcing the surviving prisoners on brutal death marches south. Nisei soldiers on patrol encountered hundreds of starving prisoners who had been left for dead. They tried to get them food and shelter as best they could. Deeply disturbed by what they had seen, the soldiers marched on to join other Allied forces at the "Eagle's Nest," Hitler's hideaway. Days later, the war ended and the nisei were finally on their way back home.

In 1943, the US government began allowing more nisei to leave the incarceration camps. Young men joined the military, and women, like Monica Itoi, were needed to fill the many jobs that had been left vacant because of the war. But Japanese Americans were still forbidden from returning to the West Coast. And so Monica headed to Chicago, to be a dentist's assistant.

Later that year, Monica finally got her long-delayed wish to go to college, where she studied literature and writing. During her second year, her parents urged her to come spend Christmas with them. And so she packed up and took a train back to their camp at Minidoka.

Japanese American soldier with the 522nd Field Artillery Battalion stands next to a concentration camp survivor he has just liberated on a death march from Dachau in May 1945.

FRED KOREMATSU

While Japanese American soldiers were fighting on the front lines of battles overseas, others were fighting for their rights at home. When twenty-three-year-old Fred Korematsu's family was forced to relocate from their home in San Leandro, California, in 1942, he refused to go with them. He was discovered by authorities and arrested.

"I didn't feel guilty because I didn't do anything wrong," Korematsu later explained. "Every day in school, we said the pledge of the flag 'with liberty and justice for all,' and I believed that. I was an American citizen, and I had as many rights as anyone else." Korematsu was convicted of defying a military order and was sent to the Topaz Relocation Center in Utah.

Fred Korematsu

From there, he appealed his conviction, and the case went all the way to the Supreme Court. In December 1944, the court issued its ruling. They decided that the incarceration of Japanese Americans did *not* violate the US Constitution. Justice Hugo Black (who was a former member of the Ku Klux Klan), delivered the majority opinion. The forced removal of Japanese Americans was a "military necessity," and so it should be allowed.

A great thing about this nation is that anyone can take their case to the highest court in our land.

But the court doesn't always get things right.

Today, the *Korematsu v. United States* case is widely viewed as a shameful mistake. In fact, the Justice Department later admitted that government lawyers had deliberately misled the Supreme

Court about the security threat posed by Japanese Americans.

Japanese Americans could not forget the way they had been treated. Activists pressed for justice for decades. In 1988, Congress and then-president Ronald Reagan signed the Civil Liberties Act, which issued a national apology for the treatment of Japanese Americans during World War II. The act set aside $20,000 for each surviving family affected by the mass incarceration.

The payments didn't come close to making up for the losses faced by Japanese Americans. The physical and mental scars of the mass incarceration would stay with them their entire lives, and would continue to be carried by the next generation of their descendants.

Walking back into Minidoka was like entering a ghost town. With the young men off fighting, and the other nisei working in the Midwest or East Coast, it was too quiet. The older issei still hoped to return to their former lives and businesses on the West Coast. They waited, not knowing for sure if the government would lift its restrictions against Japanese Americans at the war's end, or if they would forever be forbidden from returning to their homes.

When Monica's holiday was over, her parents walked her to the camp gate to say goodbye. Her mother told her that she was happy that Monica had found her place and seemed to be doing so well despite all they had gone through. "When the war came and we were all evacuated, Papa and I were heartsick," she told her daughter. "We felt terribly bad about being your Japanese parents."

Monica, who used to resent going to Japanese school, who had once felt stuck—neither American enough nor Japanese enough—rushed to comfort her mother. "No, don't say those things, Mama, please," she said. "I don't resent my Japanese blood anymore. I'm proud of it, in fact, because of you and the Issei who've struggled so much for us."

In December 1944, the War Relocation Authority signed off on the closures of all the camps. Monica's parents and others still living in the barracks were finally free to leave and start trying to pick up the pieces of their lives. The US government would not issue an apology for the atrocities committed against Japanese Americans for another forty years.

And justice may never have come if it had not been for the hard work of a new generation of Japanese Americans who would grow up in a new era of civil rights, activism, and solidarity.

IMPOSSIBLE DREAMS: DEANN BORSHAY

Deann Borshay was in college when she began having impossible dreams.

Up until that point, Deann had lived a life that seemed happy and carefree. She had supportive parents and loving siblings. She was a high school cheerleader, homecoming queen, and class president. Born in South Korea, Deann had been adopted by the Borshays from an orphanage in 1966 when she was nine years old and arrived in the US as Cha Jung Hee.

At first, she struggled to adjust to her new life in California. But after a little while, she settled in, learned to speak English, and began to meld seamlessly into the Borshay family. It helped that the Borshays loved Deann so completely. From the moment they met her at the airport, they had taken her into their hearts as their own child.

Deann was eager to be a good daughter, and she wanted to tell her parents the truth. Once she learned enough English to

Deann's first night in the United States with her adoptive mother, Alveen Borshay, March 1966.

communicate, she tried to explain to her mom that she had a family back in Korea: a mother, brother, and sisters. Deann's mom assured her that it couldn't be true. They had papers from the orphanage in Korea showing that Deann's mother had died during childbirth, and she was an orphan.

And so Deann began to forget where she had lived in Korea. She forgot how to speak Korean. And she forgot her Korean name.

It was not until she went away from home to attend college that Deann's life in Korea started to come back to her. And she realized that the impossible dreams she was having—dreams of Korean family members, of real places where she had walked and played—were not dreams at all. They were long-buried memories.

Deann picked up a pen and wrote to the orphanage where her parents had adopted her from. She received a letter in return that told her the truth—a truth she had once known but had forced herself to forget.

That letter sparked Deann's quest to understand the full scope of her own life story. The journey would take her back to Korea, a country that had been rocked by long years of colonialism and war and shaped by the ambitions of other nations—including the United States.

When World War II ended, European colonial powers began pulling out of Asia.

The US and its European allies, including the Soviet Union, had won the war, but not before Japan had dealt significant blows to the British and French in Asia. At the same time, long-standing calls for independence by Asian nations were reaching a roar. In India, for example, activists like Mahatma Gandhi had called for South Asia to be free of British rule. The end of the war provided the opportunity for this dream to become real.

But the retreat of its European allies from Asia made the US uneasy. For centuries, it was Europe that had held power over much of South and Southeast Asia. Now, with Europe devastated by the war, who would fill the role of power on the continent? Would it be China? Would it be the Soviet Union?

Or maybe it should be the United States? After all, the US had emerged from the war with a powerful and large military. This victory was an opportunity to have a say in how the future would unfold in Asia.

The letter that Deann Borshay received from the orphanage confirmed what she had tried to explain as a little girl: She was not an orphan at all. She had a mother and siblings still living in Korea. And her real Korean name was not even Cha Jung Hee, as printed on her adoption papers. It was Kang Ok Jin.

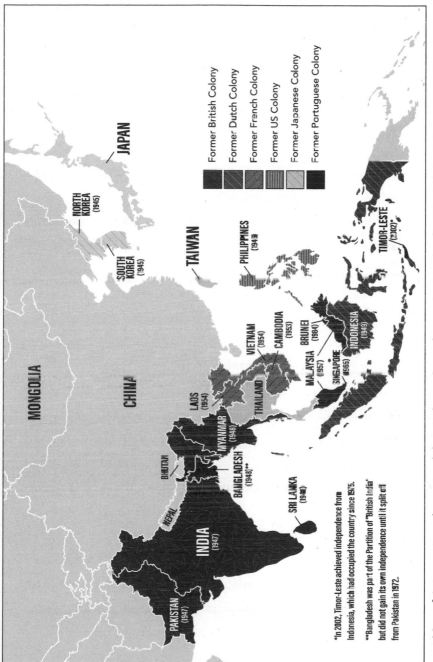

Map of Asian nations that gained their independence from colonial rule after World War II. For some nations, independence was only achieved after years, and sometimes decades, of struggle.

MONGOLIA

CHINA

JAPAN

NORTH KOREA (1945)

SOUTH KOREA (1945)

TAIWAN

PHILIPPINES (1946)

Former British Colony
Former Dutch Colony
Former French Colony
Former US Colony
Former Japanese Colony
Former Portuguese Colony

VIETNAM (1954)

CAMBODIA (1953)

BRUNEI (1984)

INDONESIA (1949)

MALAYSIA (1957)

SINGAPORE (1965)

THAILAND

LAOS (1954)

MYANMAR (1948)

BHUTAN

NEPAL

BANGLADESH (1948)**

SRI LANKA (1948)

INDIA (1947)

PAKISTAN (1947)

TIMOR-LESTE (2002)*

*In 2002, Timor-Leste achieved independence from Indonesia, which had occupied the country since 1975.

**Bangladesh was part of the Partition of "British India" but did not gain its own independence until it split off from Pakistan in 1972.

When Deann learned the truth—that the orphanage had lied to the Borshays and falsified documents that passed Deann off as a different Korean girl—it brought back a swell of hidden memories. "When I was younger I think I held on to this fantasy that if I was good enough in my new home and good enough with my American parents, that if everything was perfect and if I behaved properly and did well in school, that I would somehow be sent back to Korea to be with my Korean family."

Confronting the truth of her past left Deann shocked and heartbroken. So much had been taken from her: her family, her heritage. "I had been given a history and an identity that didn't belong to me."

How could such a thing happen?

War brings suffering, death, and destruction.

It is harshest on the most vulnerable, which often means that women and children suffer the most. For Deann's birth mother, as it was for many Koreans, life was a constant struggle. Korea had endured thirty-five years of harsh Japanese colonial rule. When Japan surrendered to the allied powers on August 15, 1945, Koreans expected to regain their independence. They expected peace. But peace was not to be.

Tensions between the United States and its former ally the Soviet Union were ramping up quickly. Both nations wanted to control what happened in the newly independent Korea. Shortly after Japan surrendered, the United States proposed dividing Korea in two at the 38th parallel. The Soviet Union accepted this proposal. The

A Korean girl and her brother in front of a stalled M46 tank at Haengju, Korea. June 9, 1951.

Korean people were not given a say in the matter.

There were now two Koreas: an anti-communist dictatorship in the south backed by the United States and its allies, and a communist government in the north backed by the Soviet Union and, later, China. The creation of two separate states led to frequent border clashes along the 38th parallel and, eventually, full-blown fighting.

This bloody civil war was also an international struggle for power in Asia. Fifteen United Nations member states joined a US-led military coalition in support of South Korea, while North Korea was aided by Soviet weaponry and Chinese equipment and troops. In just three years, the Korean War claimed approximately 4 million lives.

The Korean War came to a stalemate in 1953, but a formal

peace agreement was never signed. Korea remains divided at the Demilitarized Zone (DMZ), near the 38th parallel. The war technically continues to this day.

Deann's Korean family survived the Korean War, but when she was three years old, her father died. Now a widow with five children, Deann's mother could afford to care for her children but could not afford to send them to school. Her neighbor worked at the local orphanage and encouraged her to send her youngest daughter there, where she would be taken care of and given an education.

Many families at the time used orphanages as a kind of foster

WHY WAS IT CALLED THE COLD WAR?

When World War II ended, two nations emerged as the most dominant "superpowers": the United States and the Soviet Union. Both were big in geographical size and had powerful militaries, lots of weapons, and large economies. But those economies were based on very different principles: the United States is a capitalist nation, and the Soviet Union was communist.

Before the war even ended, competition and distrust had grown between the two powerful nations. The United States government began to fear that other countries around the world would become communist, and those countries might take sides with the US's biggest rival, the Soviet Union. US president Harry Truman, in what came to be known as the Truman Doctrine, told Congress that the US had a responsibility to defend other nations from the "threat of communist domination."

care to provide temporary support during times of hardship. Some-times parents sent children to orphanages because they knew they would get a basic education there. When the orphanage pushed for permission to release Deann (Kang Ok Jin) for adoption, her mother refused multiple times. Finally, worried that her mother would refuse again, the orphanage sent Deann abroad to the US early, without giving her family warning or a chance to say goodbye.

The Borshays had been in touch with the orphanage about wanting to adopt a different girl named Cha Jung Hee. But Cha Jung Hee went home to her family before she could be adopted.

The strategy that followed was labeled "containment." This meant that any time the Soviet Union made an aggressive move on another country or supported anti-colonial movements—in Asia or anywhere else in the world—the US would step in and push back. The reasoning was that if the US could prevent communism from spreading to other countries, then the Soviet Union would be isolated, and it would be forced to change its ways from within.

The US involvement in the Korean War, the Vietnam War, and numerous other military conflicts around the world was all a part of this strategy of containing communism. It was also an effort to establish control over other nations to benefit the interests of the United States. Because the US and the Soviet Union never actually declared war on each other, the years between 1947 and 1991 are called the Cold War. This long period of time was made even more tense for all involved because of the looming threat that either side might use its nuclear weapons on the other, unleashing catastrophic destruction for the entire globe.

The staff at the orphanage created false papers for Deann (Kang Ok Jin) that said she was Cha Jung Hee. When the Borshay family picked up Deann at the airport, they had no idea that she was not the girl they had been expecting.

American families, moved by television footage of

A group of children at the Children's Protective Home in Pusan (now known as Busan), South Korea, in 1955.

orphaned Korean children during the war, reached out to adopt them and bring them to the United States. While these adoptions began as a humanitarian response to war, the number of Korean children sent overseas continued to rise in the decades after the fighting ceased. Deann was a part of this postwar wave of adoptions.

Because the Korean War technically never ended, South Korea focused all its resources on strengthening its military and rebuilding its economy. There was no social safety net for women like Deann's Korean mother. Instead of developing programs to help families in poverty or address overpopulation, South Korea began to rely on international adoption as a way to handle these issues. Corruption within the system led to false records, switched identities, and the erased pasts of thousands of Korean children—like Kang Ok Jin.

The adoption system became like a machine. Eventually, 200,000 Korean children would be funneled into the machinery and sent overseas.

Deann Borshay returned to Korea in her twenties. She reunited with her mother, her brother, and her sisters. Later, Deann brought her American mom and dad to Korea to meet her Korean family. Despite the language barriers, these reunions and meetings were loving and full of emotion. They were also painful and complicated. There were moments of shared understanding in the face of unexplainable sorrows. And moments of realizing that there are some things that may never be understood.

"You hope that retracing your roots will give you some answers, but it only leads to more questions," writes Lisa Wool-Rim

Sjöblom, who also journeyed to Korea to uncover the truth of her own adoption and meet her living birth parents. The stories of Deann and Lisa raise many questions, not just for them, but about international adoption itself.

What pressures force birth parents to relinquish their children to adoption agencies? And are these decisions really made of their own free will? How will the adopted child adjust to their new life? How does it affect them to grow up removed from their culture, language, and society? Could the money spent on international adoption be better invested in supporting children and their families in their home countries?

Confronting these questions, Deann created an award-winning film, *First Person Plural*, which documented her incredible personal journey to Korea.

"My childhood fantasy of returning to my family is starting to get away from me," she says at the end of the film. "And I have to develop another relationship, a different kind of relationship, with my Korean family."

Through interviews and home movies, Deann shows how she and her family try to reconcile the pain of lost time. She reveals the impossible choices that war and its aftermath force human beings to make. The film is evidence of the many ways Asian Americans are connected to their countries of origin, to their ancestors, and to the twists and turns of history. But it is also a reminder of the costs of war and how even humanitarian efforts can lead to unexpected consequences and even more loss.

FROM PICTURE BRIDES TO PUNK ROCKERS: ASIAN AMERICAN WOMEN MAKE HISTORY

Early US immigration laws sought to shut out Asian women from entering America. Despite the many challenges facing them, women have found ways to immigrate, to build and sustain their families and communities, and to change what it means to be American.

PICTURE PERFECT

In the early 1900s, as more Japanese immigrant men worked in the US and saved up their money, they began to think about settling down. Because few women had immigrated with them, and because of the laws against interracial marriage in the US, they looked for wives back in Japan. First, they sought help from their parents, relatives, and even matchmakers. Then they sent photos of themselves to be shared with prospective wives.

Just as people today choose their best selfies to post online, Japanese immigrants a century ago dressed in their best clothes, went to photography studios, and sent photos of themselves back home. Sometimes, they posed in front of fancy cars or nice houses that were not their own, or they paid the photographer extra to touch up the photos—their version of a social media filter. Some of the letters they sent back with the photos exaggerated their wealth and status in the US.

Many Japanese women answered the call to immigrate. Some, with few prospects at home, were eager to begin a new adventure overseas. Others reluctantly followed their parents' wishes. Between 1908 and 1920, 20,000 Japanese "picture brides" traveled to Hawai'i and the mainland.

Clutching their photographs in their hands, the young women scanned the crowd on the docks. Some collapsed in shock if the photo they held of a handsome young man didn't match the reality standing before them! For many, the cruelest disappointment lay in the harsh life ahead of them: backbreaking work on Hawaiian sugar plantations or West Coast farms, homesickness, and discrimination. Other women stepped off the docks toward fulfilling marriages and family life.

Japanese picture brides at Angel Island, California, in 1910.

WAR'S LASTING SHADOW

After the United States dropped its atomic bombs on the cities of Hiroshima and Nagasaki in 1945, Japan lay in ruins. The once-feared empire had its military disbanded, and the United States army occupied the country for ten years—the only time in Japan's history that it has been occupied by a foreign power. That occupation brought 400,000 to 600,000 US soldiers into the country.

In the decades after World War II, nearly 67,000 Japanese women came to the US as wives of servicemen. Nearly 100,000 Korean women also immigrated during these years. Once here, women worked to bring their other family members to America.

Interracial marriages between US servicemen and their "war brides" weren't always welcomed—on either side of the Pacific. Some Japanese families objected to the point of disowning their daughters. The US Army discouraged interracial marriage, and many states still outlawed marriage between whites and non-whites (the Supreme Court would not rule these marriage bans unconstitutional until 1967). And because of immigration laws, most women who did immigrate were still not allowed to become naturalized citizens.

American soldiers were being stationed not just in Japan but all over Asia, with military bases and soldiers in Thailand, Taiwan, Korea, and the Philippines. Wherever they went, American soldiers brought American culture, music, and goods with them.

Compared to the Asian countries that had been battered by war, the United States seemed modern, powerful, and wealthy.

Throughout Asia, the areas around military bases became important economic hubs for local people whose livelihoods had been upended by the war. Stores and restaurants popped up where American soldiers could go to spend their powerful American dollars. Seedier establishments like bars and dance halls also sprang up to cater to the young soldiers' desires.

The Asian women who met and began romances with American men in these environments were often shadowed by personal tragedy. Many had lost friends and family in the war. Others struggled to find work and survive in economies that had been completely shattered.

Because of the strange balance of power that existed around military bases, a stereotypical vision of the Asian woman was formed: they were meek, eager to please, and eager to enter into romantic relationships with white men. These harmful stereotypes, made worse by Hollywood and the media, followed Asian women as they immigrated to the US, where the stereotypes still linger and do harm to this day.

TELLING THEIR OWN STORIES

Starting in the middle of the twentieth century, movies and television began to portray Asian women on-screen—and they almost always got it wrong. Even talented, barrier-breaking actresses like Anna

May Wong and Nancy Kwan had a hard time reaching beyond the stereotyped roles created for them. Who was the Asian American woman? For decades, Hollywood offered a few offensive answers: she was either passive and subservient, or exotic and seductive, or ruthless and deceitful—a "dragon lady."

The 2018 film *To All the Boys I've Loved Before* (starring actress Lana Condor, left), based on the bestselling novel by Jenny Han (right), broke barriers as the first teen romantic comedy to star an Asian American female lead.

Stereotypes can be sticky and hard to shake. Even today, offensive ideas about Asian and Asian American women persist. But women like comedians Awkwafina and Mindy Kaling, authors Sabaa Tahir and Laura Gao, and musicians Olivia Rodrigo and Jhené Aiko are pushing back against stereotypes by portraying themselves in layered, multidimensional ways. Who is the Asian American woman? There is no one answer. She is everything, and she is telling her own story.

The Linda Lindas performing at Rock im Park in Nuremberg, Germany, 2022. The performers were teenagers when they formed their all-girl rock band.

14

SOLIDARITY: THE ONGOING FIGHT FOR CIVIL RIGHTS

While Monica Itoi's family was being "evacuated" from Seattle in 1942, another Japanese American family was being ripped apart 1,000 miles to the south, in San Pedro, California.

On the day Pearl Harbor was attacked, Mary Yuriko (Yuri) Nakahara was twenty years old and had been teaching Sunday school at her church. She hurried home to help take care of her father, who had just gotten out of the hospital from ulcer surgery. Yuri's father was a fisherman, and rumors were swirling that Japanese fishermen were spying for Japan to give them maps of the US coastline. A few minutes after Yuri arrived at home, FBI agents showed up at the door, demanding to see her father. They pulled him out of bed in his weakened state and took him away. He was treated poorly during his two-month interrogation. When he was finally allowed to come home, he died the next day.

Yuri and her surviving family spent the war years incarcerated at a prison camp in Jerome, Arkansas. There, she witnessed how

Jim Crow segregation of the South kept African Americans as second-class citizens. The injustices she saw committed against African Americans sparked something in her: anger, but also a feeling that she should do something to fight against inequality. After the war ended, Yuri married a young Japanese American man named Bill Kochiyama, who had served in the famous Fighting 442nd Regimental Combat Team, and the couple moved to New York City. It was there that those activist embers would blaze into life.

Yuri Kochiyama (born Mary Nakahara), far left wearing glasses, with a group of children at the incarceration camp in Jerome, Arkansas, during World War II.

Yuri soon met Daisy Bates, an African American civil rights activist who had guided the "Little Rock Nine": the first African American students to enroll in the segregated Little Rock Central High School in Arkansas. After meeting Daisy, "I began to take a serious interest in the civil rights movement," Kochiyama said. "People were fighting for things that we had taken for granted. . . . I started to realize that I needed to fight for my civil rights, too."

In the 1950s and 1960s, African Americans cried out for racial justice. They were organizing bus boycotts in Alabama, sit-ins at restaurant counters in North Carolina, and all over the South, "Freedom Riders," Black and white activists, boarded buses together to protest segregation.

In 1958, Mildred Loving, a woman of African and Native American descent, and Richard Loving, a white man, were arrested simply for being married. Their case went all the way to the Supreme Court, and in 1967, the court struck down all laws banning interracial marriage.

Generations of Asian Americans had been prevented from having families and building happy lives because of laws that forbade them to marry outside their race. Now, thanks to the fight of Mildred and Richard Loving, that would be forever changed.

The fight for African American civil rights inspired and energized activists of all races. Asian Americans like Yuri Kochiyama were ready to work with each other and with others for political power, for their rights, and for equality. It was time to build a new America.

Bayard Rustin was the chief organizer of the 1963 March on Washington, where Dr. Martin Luther King, Jr., made his landmark "I have a dream" speech. Rustin was a passionate speaker and activist, who was discriminated against because he was African

American and because he was openly gay at a time in history when homophobia was rampant. He was a champion for civil rights in both the US and in Asia, where he joined those calling for Indian independence.

He learned the strategies of peaceful protest firsthand from Mahatma Gandhi's colleagues in the 1940s. Rustin and his colleagues then passed on the techniques of nonviolent protest to activists like Dr. King. After meeting with the peace activist Buddhist monk Thich Nhat Hanh, Dr. King began to speak out against American involvement in the Vietnam War. After the war in Vietnam, Rustin met with refugees from Southeast Asia. At a time when some Americans were arguing that the refugees should not be allowed in, Rustin organized African American civil rights leaders to advocate on their behalf. "Black people must recognize these people for what they are: brothers and sisters."

Grace Lee Boggs grew up in Providence, Rhode Island, the daughter of Chinese immigrant parents. She went to college and even received her PhD. But no college or university would hire her. She moved to Chicago, where she saw how African American activists were able to change things, such as fair hiring practices, by working together. "When I saw what a movement could do I said, 'Boy, that's what I wanna do with my life,'" Grace recalled.

She married African American activist James Boggs and they moved to Detroit. The couple worked together for decades on issues of civil rights, Black Power, labor, women's rights, environmental concerns, antiwar movements, and Asian American rights.

Activist Grace Lee Boggs, 2012.

The fight for racial equality extended from cities and college campuses to America's farm fields.

Larry Itliong had come to the United States from the Philippines when he was just fifteen years old. He had worked as a laborer all his life, in canneries up and down the West Coast, and following the fruit and vegetable harvests as a migrant farmworker. Larry was a born leader, who taught himself law by sitting in on trials and paying attention. Larry devoted his life to forming unions and leading strikes in order to protect the rights of his fellow Filipino brothers in the field.

Larry's path eventually intersected with that of another rising leader in the Filipino American community: Philip Vera Cruz. In

Itliong organized thousands of laborers for the Agricultural Workers Organizing Committee and United Farm Workers.

1948, Philip had been part of an important strike of asparagus farmworkers that protested the low wages and poor conditions of the labor camps. Philip described their bleak situation: "The first camp I lived in had a kitchen that was so full of holes, flies were just coming in and out. . . . The toilet was an outhouse with the pit so full that it was impossible to use."

Larry and Phillip knew that growers used workers of different races against each other to prevent anyone from getting rights. For example, if a group of Korean farmworkers would strike to improve their working conditions, the farm owners would truck in Mexican workers to do the job instead. These tactics prevented every worker from getting the rights they all deserved.

On September 7, 1965, Filipino grape workers gathered in the Filipino Community Hall in Delano, California, to organize a strike for higher wages. Larry warned the workers that the strike could be long and it could get violent. Farm owners would regularly respond to strikes by beating the striking workers, or going into their camps and turning off the water or electricity.

Larry and Philip knew that they would never be successful if the farm owners turned to Mexican workers to fill their places. They approached Mexican American labor leaders Dolores Huerta and Cesar Chavez. The leaders agreed that only by working together would they achieve the gains their people needed. Mexican Americans joined the Filipino American grape strike. They formed the joint organization the United Farm Workers Organizing Committee, which worked to gain international attention for the strike. People of all races all over America refused to buy grapes until the farmworkers were given a raise. In 1970, the farm owners finally broke down and signed an agreement with the laborers, ending the strike.

Like the striking farmworkers, Yuri Kochiyama also believed that interracial solidarity was the only way to change the future for all Americans. Yuri tirelessly pressed the US government to make reparations for its incarceration of Japanese Americans during World War II. In the 1970s, Yuri marched with Puerto Ricans at the Statue of Liberty to call for Puerto Rico's independence. And throughout her life, Yuri served as a bridge between Asian Americans and activists of other races, including Malcolm X, the prominent African American activist who pushed for Black Power within the African American community.

In February of 1965, Malcolm X was in New York City, preparing to give a speech to a ballroom with a full audience. Someone began shouting, and in the chaos that followed, a gunman shot Malcolm X in the chest. As most of the audience fell to the floor and tried to stay out of the range of gunfire, Kochiyama headed toward Malcolm X. As he lay dying, she cradled the civil rights leader's head in her lap. "I said, 'Please, Malcolm! Please, Malcolm! Stay alive!'" But it was too late.

Racist violence like Malcolm X's assassination emboldened America's enemies to criticize democracy. Communist countries like the Soviet Union said that the injustices in the US proved that America was just a big hypocrite.

At meetings of the United Nations, when American diplomats tried to bring up human rights abuses by the Soviet Union, they would be met with the reply, "Well, in your country, you are lynching African Americans." Racism in America made it awfully hard to conduct foreign affairs abroad. The argument was, how could the United States expect to be a world leader if it was repressing the rights of its own citizens?

And so what was the United States going to be? Was it going to be the country that had been founded on the promises of equality, justice, and freedom? Was it going to walk the walk, and pass some laws that actually made these promises come true for everyone?

Across the country in the 1960s, these questions would be put to the test.

AMERICA'S GATES REOPEN: THE 1965 IMMIGRATION AND NATIONALITY ACT

In the spring of 1979, Chih-Wei Chou was sitting in the principal's office of her new middle school.

She wasn't in trouble. She was there to pick a new name.

Until just a few days before, Chih-Wei had been a middle school student in her hometown of Taipei, Taiwan. Several of her mother's siblings were living in the US at the time, and her mom's visa paperwork had just been approved. The decision to move was so quick that Chih-Wei didn't even have time to say goodbye to her classmates.

But she was too excited to be sad. On the plane ride over the Pacific Ocean, she pressed every button within reach and cleaned her dinner tray so completely that the flight attendants started serving her two meals. Everything was amazing. They were going to America! Chih-Wei wondered if her new hometown would look anything like a popular American television show that played on Taiwanese television: *Little House on the Prairie*.

When they landed in Los Angeles, California, Chih-Wei and her mother moved in with her mother's brother and his kids. The treelined neighborhood with its manicured lawns was nothing like the prairie she had imagined, and totally different from the high-rise buildings back in Taipei. They were the only Asian family in the area, but the neighbors were friendly, and the kids seemed nice.

There was only one problem: Chih-Wei spoke very little English. And so, as she sat in the principal's office that morning, she had to wait for her mother to translate the principal's words for her:

Would she like to have an English name to use at school?

While there are many instances where immigrants have been pressured to change their names to sound "more American" or change the spelling to make it easy for English speakers to pronounce, this was not the case for Chih-Wei. She was excited to choose a new American name. But what should it be?

The principal threw out some suggestions, before offering, "How about 'Wendy'?"

Wendy. Like the girl from *Peter Pan*. Yes, that was perfect.

And so, Wendy Chou dove headfirst into her new life in a new school in her new country with a new name. With her limited English, almost every class except for math was bewildering, and other students were assigned to talk with her so that she could practice her conversation skills.

Those early days must have been lonely, but Wendy was far from alone. She was one of the many young people who were making the move from Asian countries to start new lives in the United States.

After nearly a century of shutting out non-white, non-European immigrants, America had finally started to open its gates.

Wendy Chou (Le) and her mother (both wearing flower garlands) with friends who came to say goodbye at the airport on the day they immigrated to the US from Taiwan.

Wendy's move to the US was made possible by a new law that had been passed a few years earlier: the 1965 Immigration and Nationality Act. When President Lyndon B. Johnson signed the bill into law, standing in the New York City sunshine with the Statue of Liberty in the background, he gave these remarks:

This bill we sign today is not a revolutionary bill. It does not affect the lives of millions. It will not restructure the shape of our daily lives.

That's kind of an odd thing for a president to say about a law they just signed. Most of the time, presidents like to brag about how historic the moment is, and how much their actions are going to change things. But Johnson had his reasons for downplaying it.

During his two years as president, he had already signed some of the most significant legislation in US history, including the 1964 Civil Rights Act, which made it illegal to discriminate against someone based on race, color, religion, sex, or nationality. Just two months prior, he had signed the historic Voting Rights Act into law, which outlawed discrimination that had been used to keep African Americans from voting.

Through marching, protesting, petitioning, and putting their own lives on the line, African American civil rights activists had pressed the American public and their president to make changes toward a more just and equal America.

President Johnson and other leaders in the US saw the new immigration act as an extension of the civil rights legislation they had passed. They pointed out that this new immigration law would undo the decades of discriminatory policies that had shut out so many. It would be fair, and it would make good on the promise of America that everyone should be equal. But the president was also quick to assure folks that even though the law was a great thing, *nothing major was going to change*. He did this because he knew that plenty of people were not going to like it.

The same people who opposed civil rights for African Americans also pushed back against any changes to immigration. They claimed that without race-based immigration barriers, America would be overrun by "hordes" of Africans or Asians, or become a "dumping ground" for migrants from Latin America.

There are too many of them.

Opponents to immigration argued that if the United States opened its doors to more immigrants, the country would become less white. For them, America was a white country, and it should stay that way.

President Lyndon B. Johnson signs the 1965 Immigration and Nationality Act.

For decades, US immigration law had excluded immigrants based on a person's race or where they were from. During the 1930s and into World War II, American lawmakers would not even change the rules to allow Jewish refugees into the country to escape extermination by the Nazis. Only a small number were able to enter. And in fact, Nazi Germany's leader, Adolf Hitler himself, admired the racism of America's immigration laws. They excluded the "foreign body" of "strangers to the blood" of the ruling (Nordic-German) race, he wrote in an unpublished sequel to *Mein Kampf*. He commended the US for its actions.

When Hitler is praising your immigration laws, it's not a great sign.

President John F. Kennedy tried to advocate for immigration reform and even celebrated America's heritage of immigration in his 1958 book *A Nation of Immigrants*. But he was assassinated before he could make his dream of a new immigration law a reality. President Johnson vowed to follow through on the slain president's agenda. He faced a lot of opposition in Congress. One of the conservative leaders who didn't want to change the immigration law was Representative Michael Feighan from Ohio. Feighan reluctantly agreed to vote for the bill, but he insisted on a key change.

He wanted the law to give preference to people who already had family living in the United States. He reasoned that since most of the immigrants already in the US were from Europe, this would tilt things in favor of white, European nations. But Feighan miscalculated.

What he hadn't counted on was that in the decades to follow, fewer Europeans would want to move to America—even if they already had family there. But for people living in Asia, Africa, and Latin America, the desire to migrate was growing stronger. By 2010, family-based immigration made up about three-fourths of all immigration. And most of those people were coming from countries that Feighan and his colleagues had intended to keep out.

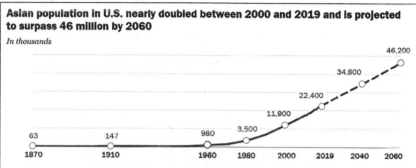

Asian population in U.S. nearly doubled between 2000 and 2019 and is projected to surpass 46 million by 2060

In thousands

63	147		980	3,500	11,900	22,400	34,800	46,200
1870	1910		1960	1980	2000	2019	2040	2060

Note: In 2000 and later, Asians include the mixed-race and mixed-group populations, regardless of Hispanic origin. Prior to 2000, decennial census forms only allowed one race category to be selected. Asians include Pacific Islanders in 1980 and earlier years. Population figures for 1870-1980 are rounded to the nearest 1,000, and for 2000-2060, they are rounded to the nearest 100,000.
Source: U.S. Census Bureau 2017 population projections for 2020-2060. For 2011-2019, American Community Survey 1-year estimates (via Census Bureau data). For 2000 and 2010, census counts from Census Bureau, "The Asian Population: 2010" Census Brief, Table 6. For 1990, U.S. Census Bureau, "Asian Population: 2000" Census Brief, Table 2. For 1980 and earlier years, Campbell Gibson and Kay Jung, "Historical Census Statistics on Population Totals by Race, 1790 to 1990, and by Hispanic Origin, 1970 to 1990, for the United States, Regions, Divisions and States." U.S. Census Bureau.

PEW RESEARCH CENTER

As this graph shows, the Asian population in the US rose dramatically after the 1965 Immigration and Nationality Act was passed and continues to grow. It nearly doubled between 2000 and 2019. The law also increased the diversity of Asian Americans. Before 1965, Chinese and Japanese Americans made up the largest share of the Asian American population. Today, Indian Americans, Chinese Americans, Filipino Americans, and Vietnamese Americans are among the largest.

The new law changed where immigrants were coming from. Before 1960, Japanese Americans were the largest Asian American group, making up 50 percent of all Asian Americans. After 1965, people began arriving from countries in Asia that had sent very few immigrants to the US before: Taiwan, Thailand, Vietnam, Laos, Pakistan, Cambodia, and Bangladesh.

After 1965, more female immigrants began arriving in the US, and many immigrants arrived as families. Before, when laws prevented foreign-born immigrants from becoming citizens, many people would return to their home countries. Now they stayed.

Family-based immigration after 1965 became such a big feature of the new law that it was even nicknamed the "Brothers and Sisters Act."

Author Christina Soontornvat's father (left) and uncle (right), with a cousin at the Bangkok airport on the day they immigrated to the United States from Thailand in 1967. Christina's uncle obtained his visa to study law at an American university. The 1965 Immigration and Nationality Act removed race-based quotas of previous immigration laws. In addition to giving preference to immigrants who already had family living in the US, the law favored professionals or those with specialized skills.

Wendy Chou's mother's visa had been sponsored by her older sister, who had moved to the US years before to get a PhD in chemistry. Over time, she sponsored visas not just for Wendy and Wendy's mom, but for eleven of her twelve siblings, eventually bringing her own mother over from Taiwan as well. The 1965 law changed the trajectory for almost their entire family. In turn, Wendy's family—along with many others—helped to rewrite the story of what it means to be American.

As Wendy finished middle school and then started high school, her English skills got better and better. Soon, she even dreamed in English. The move to the US had made her adaptable. She had lots of friends from all kinds of different backgrounds, and she flitted easily between social groups at school.

In tenth grade, her social studies teacher asked for a volunteer from the class to recite the Pledge of Allegiance. Everyone else was too shy, so Wendy raised her hand. She recited it perfectly.

"See there?" the teacher said. "Wendy wasn't even born here and look how well she did."

The comment made Wendy realize that even though she wasn't born in the US, at some point over the years, she had become American. There was no singular moment when it happened. She just . . . was. When her application for US citizenship was approved at the age of eighteen, it seemed more like a formality than a turning point in her life. She faced the flag, raised her right hand, and spoke the pledge (which, of course, she already knew by heart).

Wendy went on to college, majoring in a new and exciting field called computer science. She married and had a son.

And then one day, a teacher at her son's school asked for Wendy's help. They had two new students from China who barely spoke English, and they needed to communicate something to them. As Wendy translated for the children (who luckily also spoke Mandarin, Wendy's home dialect), she had the bizarre sensation of being pulled back through time. She had once been in these students' very same shoes, and now here she was, acting as their American translator.

When she was finished speaking to the children, she smiled at them and thought, *You are going to be just fine. Trust me.*

There is a poem inscribed on the inside of the pedestal of the Statue of Liberty, written by Emma Lazarus, which renames Lady Liberty the "Mother of Exiles" and describes how:

From her beacon-hand glows world-wide welcome.

For decades, this colossal symbol of America's compassion seemed to only welcome white, Christian immigrants from Europe. The "world-wide welcome" had not applied to immigrants from Asia, most of whom attempted to enter the US through Angel Island.

The 1965 Immigration Act helped to make those words true for many more people from around the world. The law changed the trajectory for so many Asian Americans and changed the way Asians in America were perceived. In the past century of Asian immigration, they had been given so many different labels: undesirable, unable to assimilate, exotic, dangerous, inferior, dirty, untrustworthy, Orientals.

Now, a new label would begin to rise above all the others. This label would have been a big surprise to those who had come to America in the decades before.

Asian Americans were about to be deemed the "model minority."

ASIAN AMERICAN FOOD

Today, Americans have access to a glorious feast of foods from all over Asia: dim sum and adobo, pho and bulgogi, khao soi and samosas, biryani and hot pot, and, of course, gallons of boba tea. If your mouth is watering at the mention of this scrumptious array, you can thank the 1965 Immigration Act for increasing the variety of edible treasures available in this country. But despite this joyous boon of culinary delight, the origins of Asian food in America is traced through the history of its people, which means that it began with exclusion.

During the Chinese Exclusion era, it was really difficult for a Chinese person to travel home to China and then be allowed to reenter America (until Wong Kim Ark's Supreme Court victory, that was true even if that person had been born on American soil). A loophole in the law made an exception for a small number of Chinese business owners who were allowed to return to China and bring Chinese employees with them back to America. In 1915, restaurant owners were added to this list.

In that decade, the number of Chinese restaurants in the US doubled, and then doubled again the next decade. For many

Award-winning Hmong American chef Yia Vang stands in front of the Union Hmong Kitchen food stand at the Minnesota State Fair, 2022.

Chinese immigrants—and later, immigrants from all over Asia—restaurants were the only places where they could work. But they also provided a way to start a new life in America.

A restaurant is the type of business that a family can run together. Children, aunts, uncles, and distant cousins might all be employed at the restaurant at one point or another. Workers can make a living even if they have limited English proficiency. A restaurant is also a place where a new immigrant can work alongside other Asian Americans who have been in the country for a longer time. It's a place where you can get your bearings, save up money, and figure out where you want to go next.

Coauthor Erika Lee's grandparents Ben and Gladys Huie opened the New Deal Chow Mein Inn in Brooklyn, New York, in 1934. Catering to the families in its diverse neighborhood, it offered Chinese American favorites like chow mein and chop suey. But it also featured Cantonese classics like dow see pi guot, Cantonese spareribs, and "American" dishes like chicken salad and french fries. Their New Deal wontons were particularly famous, and the Huie daughters, May (seated) and Fay and Mary (standing, left to right), made the restaurant's egg rolls after school every day.

Coauthor Christina Soontornvat at her family's restaurant in 1984 with her uncle and three of the Thai American wait staff.

Today, immigrants in America own 29 percent of all restaurants and hotels, according to the US Census. These businesses are most likely to be concentrated in cities with large immigrant communities, but they are also spread out in every pocket of the country (to the delight of taste buds everywhere).

THE MYTHICAL MODEL MINORITY

For hundreds of years, Asians in America had fought against racist labels and ideas that fueled discrimination and violence:

They were inferior.

or

They were dangerous.

or

There were too many of them.

But after the Cold War, perceptions about Asian Americans shifted dramatically.

After a century of discrimination, Asian Americans could finally become citizens, own property, vote, and marry who they wanted. And with the 1965 Immigration Act in place, Asian immigrants could come to the US more easily, reunite with their families, and start building futures for themselves. Finally, racism against Asian Americans had begun easing and they were becoming more integrated into society, into schools, and into the workplace.

But the racism did not simply go away. It evolved.

In the *Yellow Peril* painting that German Kaiser Wilhelm had commissioned and sent around the world in 1895, Asian people were shown as a terrifying horde, eager to swarm the shores and destroy the Western world. The yellow peril stereotype was based on the idea that all Asian people were a threat to the West. It was part of their nature, their biology, their race.

Beginning in the 1960s, a new and very different portrait of Asian Americans was being painted. It was a pretty picture, pleasing to the eye. In it, Asians were depicted as being quiet and law-abiding. They respected authority, they stuck to traditional gender roles (moms stayed at home and dads worked), they had stable nuclear families (a mom, a dad, and kids, all living together). They overcame obstacles. They worked hard to achieve their American Dreams and America rewarded them. They were moving up the economic ladder and into the suburbs.

The new portrait had a name: model minority.

Newspapers, television, movies, and books began to pick up on these stereotypes. They profiled Asian American kids who:

listened to their parents

were math and computer whizzes

played some sort of classical instrument

were "good," "well-behaved," "quiet," and academic.

In 1984, *Newsweek* reported that "Asian Americans pack the honor rolls of some of the country's most highly regarded schools."

Fortune magazine went further, describing Asian Americans not just as a model minority but as "America's Super Minority."

Toy Len Goon was declared "American Mother of the Year" in 1952 and given a parade in New York City's Chinatown.

According to them, Asian Americans were "smarter and better educated and make more money than everyone else" because of the way they were raised. It was Asian culture and values that emphasized education and family. "Asian Americans," the magazine declared, "are smarter than the rest of us."

At first, maybe this seems like a compliment. It's a good thing to be called smart, right? But this is one of those compliments that's actually a sneaky way of promoting racist ideas and putting someone else down. Similar to how the *Yellow Peril* painting had promoted the idea that Asians were a *threat* because of their race, the "model minority" stereotype sent the message that Asians were a *success* because of their race, their so-called Asian traits and culture. Both are racist ideas. Other minority groups in America also value family and higher education. Attributing Asian successes to something inherent to being "Asian" is similar to calling Asians a yellow peril because of their race and where they came from.

Time magazine cover from 1987.

Plus, the model minority myth is simply not true. Beginning in the 1960s, some Chinese and Japanese Americans were beginning to enjoy newfound freedoms, such as the right to become a naturalized citizen and the right to own property. They were beginning to attend college and graduate school and earning more than they had been able to before. But they were far from equal to whites, and they still faced discrimination.

Some used the model minority stereotype as an underhanded way to criticize other minorities, especially African Americans.

In the mid-1960s, thanks to the hard work of African American civil rights activists, the US had taken major steps toward creating a more equal society. The Civil Rights Act, the Voting Rights Act, and desegregation had become the law of the land. But for the fighters for racial justice, these were the *first* steps. The next steps were to alleviate poverty, make working conditions fair, and make sure African Americans could build wealth and own property, just like white Americans had been able to do for generations. There was still a lot of work left to be done.

But some people didn't want to hear about more work to do. They wanted to be finished with all this talk of change and reform. For some Americans, the attitude was, *What more do these people want?*

For those who opposed further government action on civil rights, the rising status of Asian Americans was a very convenient way to argue against doing anything for African Americans or other minorities. Just like the grape growers who had tried to pit Filipino and Mexican farmworkers against each other, these enemies of racial justice compared Asian Americans to African Americans, using one minority to hurt the other.

These opponents would point to Asian Americans and say, "If they can do it, why can't the others do it, too?" Or "See? *They're* not complaining. *They're* not protesting in the streets, calling out for 'Black Power.' *They've* achieved success the good, old-fashioned way, by pulling themselves up by their bootstraps."

The reality was that for African Americans, centuries of slavery, state-sanctioned mob violence, and Jim Crow laws had created generational poverty, disproportionate rates of incarceration, gaps in education, and drastic income inequality. Other policies like redlining, which aimed to keep minorities from buying homes in white neighborhoods, meant that the playing field was far from level for African Americans.

Remember, too, that the 1965 Immigration Act favored family members and those who were educated professionals. That meant that new Asian immigrants coming to the US after 1965 often had some stability and security when they arrived. And those with education and skills could often find good, high-paying jobs, which contributed to their upward mobility. All of this made it easier for their own kids to succeed in college and beyond.

The model minority stereotype was just another way to cover up the real truth of what was going on: the US had spent centuries enslaving Africans and taking away land and rights from Native Americans. The civil rights laws of the 1960s were important, but they could not fix things overnight. More needed to be done.

If the model minority stereotype was true, then things in the US—and its laws, its economy, and its institutions—were fine just the way they were. Asian American success proved this. If other groups were still struggling, it must be their fault.

The other reason the model minority stereotype has been such a problem is that—similarly to calling all Asians "Orientals"—it lumps all Asian Americans together, assuming that everyone is the same and ignoring important differences.

People who use the model minority myth pick and choose which Asians they hold up as models. They point to US-born and educated Chinese, Japanese, and South Asian Americans, who have higher rates of college education and earn higher salaries, while ignoring the fact that Korean Americans, Filipino Americans, Vietnamese Americans, and many others earn less on average than other American households. And even within a single group, not everyone is the same. For example, Chinese Americans represent both ends of the wealth spectrum, with 14 percent living in poverty.

The model minority stereotype has been particularly hurtful for the hundreds of thousands of Asians who came to America as refugees, fleeing persecution and violence from the wars in Southeast Asia beginning in the 1970s. Hmong, Cambodian, Laotian, and Vietnamese Americans have the lowest rates of college attendance of Asian Americans, and more live in poverty compared to the overall US population.

Southeast Asian refugees arrived in America with severe

physical and psychological trauma from the fighting and genocide they endured. Many didn't speak English, and they struggled to find jobs, go to school, and make their way in the crime-ridden neighborhoods where they were placed. This reality is not usually the way you see Asian Americans portrayed in the media. Asian Americans who don't fit the model minority mold may feel inadequate because they don't match the stereotype, when in reality it's the stereotype that needs to change.

Stereotypes are hurtful, even if they disguise themselves as compliments. The myth of the model minority hides how racial discrimination continues to be a problem for all people of color in the US. It ignores the real struggles Asian Americans have waged for equality in this country. And it diminishes the accomplishments of those Asian Americans who have fought to rise above the expectations of society.

Some of those great Americans fought their battles without ever throwing a punch—while for others, throwing punches was the name of the game.

FIRSTS AND FLYING FISTS

There is a fight scene halfway through the first episode of *The Green Hornet* television show. The scene only lasts twenty seconds, but even in that amount of time, you can tell that you are watching greatness.

The Green Hornet premiered in 1966, and it was a pretty simple superhero series that followed the successful formulas of other series like *Batman* and *Superman*. The crime-fighting Green Hornet, played by white actor Van Williams, was supposed to be the star of the show. But hundreds of fan letters that arrived every week from children all over the country were addressed to Green Hornet's Asian American sidekick, Kato.

The way Kato punched, the way he kicked, the way he simply *moved*—when he was on-screen, you couldn't take your eyes off him. Kato was played by the Chinese American actor and martial arts expert Bruce Lee. And when Bruce showed up on-screen, it was pure electricity.

Bruce Lee

The son of a Cantonese opera singer, Bruce Lee was born in San Francisco and raised in Hong Kong, where he was a child actor in several films. As a teenager, Bruce started training in martial arts and later moved to California, where he continued training and eventually opened his own martial arts studio. Bruce dedicated himself to perfecting his martial arts and creating his own style, called Jeet Kune Do. He became a masterful teacher, but he was especially known for his quicker-than-lightning speed.

In fact, when Bruce landed his acting role of Kato on *The Green Hornet*, the producers had to ask him to restrain himself during fight scenes so that he wouldn't take too much of the spotlight off the main character. Bruce agreed to shoot his Kato scenes in slow motion—because if he moved at his actual speed, it was too fast for the cameras and created a blurry image.

But when it came time to shoot a crossover show where Batman and Robin took on Green Hornet and Kato in a fight scene, Bruce refused to go along with the script, which had him losing to Robin. He walked away, saying, "There's no way that anyone would believe I go in there and fight Robin and lose." He had a point. In the end, the script was changed so that the fight ended in a draw.

Kato was many Americans' first exposure to Asian martial arts. Compared to the slug-it-out fight scenes of other Western movies, Lee's style was fresh and exciting. Bruce was full of charisma; he was strong and confident, and he was proud of his Asian heritage. For the Asian American kids watching, it felt like a revolution. For the first time, here was a character who looked like them, and it was clear that he was a superstar in every way.

Despite Bruce Lee's growing popularity, *The Green Hornet* was canceled after one season and Bruce struggled to find film roles afterward.

Hollywood films have a history of pushing racial stereotypes, and non-white actors have long battled for roles with any kind of depth. Sometimes they have even had to compete with white actors who dress in "yellowface" so they can play Asian characters. When the first Chinese American movie star, Anna May Wong, got her start in films in the 1920s and 1930s, she was always cast in supporting and stereotypically "Asian" roles. And sometimes, Wong found herself competing against white actresses who would use makeup tricks to try to make their eyes appear Asian. Wong fought against racist stereotyping in the film industry her whole career, even walking away from lead parts that she felt were beneath her dignity.

Like all Chinese Americans and Chinese immigrants in the US while the Chinese exclusion laws were in effect from 1882–1943, Anna May Wong was issued this special identification document, called a Certificate of Identity, to prove her legal residence in the US when she returned from abroad. No other ethnic group was required to have such identification documents at the time.

Like Anna May Wong, Bruce Lee wasn't going to play a racist version of a Chinese character. He wanted to make films on his own terms and be himself. So rather than bend to Hollywood's will, Lee went to Hong Kong. The vibrant Hong Kong film industry was eager to cast him in kung fu films. In Hong Kong, Lee made *Fist of Fury* and *The Way of the Dragon*, which broke box office records across Asia. In each, he was unabashedly and unapologetically himself. He was a "true Chinese man," who fought on behalf of Chinese characters on the big screen. Audiences were mesmerized by his moves and his charm, and Lee had the box office receipts to prove it. Hollywood realized they had made a big mistake, and they called to beg him to come back.

In the '60s and '70s, Bruce Lee was fighting off mobs of bad guys on the silver screen, and he was fighting for representation and ownership in the offices of Hollywood executives. At the same time, Asian Americans were also kicking butt in Washington, DC.

In 1965, Patsy Mink had become the first woman of color to serve in Congress, as the representative from the newest state in the nation: Hawai'i. As she walked the halls of the House of Representatives, other lawmakers were intrigued to see the five-foot-one Mink in their midst. A political reporter once called her "the lovely Oriental doll of a delegate from Hawai'i."

Patsy Mink would prove to them all what a mistake it was to underestimate her.

With grandparents who had toiled as plantation workers on the island of Maui, Japanese American Patsy Mink knew from an early age about the inequalities that affected the lives of most people in her home state. In most of the schools she attended as a girl, Mink was one of the only non-white students. Despite the isolation she felt, Mink thrived at school. She was a go-getter: valedictorian and class president of her high school. But when she moved to the continental US to pursue her dream of becoming a doctor, she felt like she was all alone again.

When she arrived as a freshman at a small women's college

in Pennsylvania, she was classified as a foreign student. Did they not realize that Hawai'i was a US territory and Patsy was an American? These things kept happening to her. When she transferred to the University of Nebraska in 1947, she wasn't allowed to live in the dormitories with white students, and she wasn't able to join sororities or other social organizations. "I hoped and prayed that here I could find some link with what I was told America was like," Mink wrote in a letter to the student newspaper protesting her mistreatment. "I found [the College of Medicine] polluted with germs, germs of a discriminating nature."

Patsy had big ambitions, but she continued to deal with the double discrimination of being Asian American and being a woman. Even

though she had a stellar college record, no medical school would accept her. She changed course, got married, and enrolled in the University of Chicago Law School. But again she was stymied by the prejudice of others. Law firms wouldn't hire a Japanese American. Especially not a woman. Especially not a married woman who would probably end up

Representative Patsy Mink, ca, 1965.

giving up law to have kids anyway. Patsy Mink and her husband did have children, but she wasn't giving anything up.

The Minks moved to Hawai'i, where Patsy became the first Japanese American woman in the state to practice law. Hawaiian firms wouldn't hire her (same story: Japanese American, woman, mother. Three strikes against her), so she started her own firm. She took on clients of all kinds, regardless of whether they could afford her (her first client paid her with a fish).

Patsy became very engaged in the Democratic Party in Hawai'i, putting her energy and talents toward helping to organize and get candidates elected. Over the next few years, she watched as Asian American politicians broke barriers and headed to Washington, DC.

Dalip Singh Saund as congressman, April 1, 1958.

Dalip Singh Saund had come to the US from India to earn his PhD in mathematics at UC Berkeley in 1920. But because of laws preventing him from becoming a citizen, and because of racism that kept him from putting his degree to use, he was forced to do the only work open to South Asian men—he became a farmworker. Even then, he wasn't allowed to own land, and so he formed the India Association of America to help fight for equal treatment for South Asians. When the law changed in 1946 and he was allowed to become a citizen, he decided to get into politics. During his 1956 campaign for a US House seat, Saund and his family knocked on doors and registered voters. He especially tried to reach Mexican American, African American, and Asian American voters who farmed in California's Imperial Valley. When they elected him in 1956, they sent the first Asian American to Congress. "Look at me," said Representative Saund in an emotional election night speech. "I am living proof of America's democracy."

Two years later, in 1959, Hawai'i became a state and Hawaiians elected two Asian Americans to represent them in Congress. Hawaiian voters elected Hiram Fong to the Senate, where he became the first Chinese American in Congress, and where he served as a sort of "spokesman for Asian Americans across the country."

Hawai'i also sent a World War II veteran to the House of Representatives that same year. He had witnessed the Sunday-morning bombing of Pearl Harbor, and he had enlisted the first chance he got. He had lost an arm—and very nearly lost his life—to a grenade in Italy. His name was Daniel Inouye.

Asian Americans were making political strides. Patsy Mink was ready to join them. In 1956, before Hawai'i had even achieved statehood, she ran for the Territorial House of Representatives. Her campaign goals were built from her experience as a descendant of plantation workers. She wanted to support laborers and retrieve land that had been stolen from Native Hawaiians by plantation owners and put it to use for the people of Hawai'i.

ASIAN AMERICAN LGBTQIA+ ACTIVISTS MAKE HISTORY

In the same way that Asian Americans have been hidden from history, the stories of LGBTQIA+ Americans have been left out of our nation's history books. But Asian Americans who are also LGBTQIA+ have been a part of America's story for centuries, and their contributions have made the nation a more inclusive place for all.

LGBTQIA+ Asian Americans have often felt doubly excluded: not accepted in Asian American circles, and also left out of mostly white LGBTQIA+ organizations. When a Chinese American man named Vincent Chin was murdered in a hate crime in Detroit in 1982, journalist Helen Zia leapt into action, and her activism helped to launch a nationwide movement for justice.

Asian American LGBTQIA+ activists Helen Zia and her wife, Lia Shigemura, at the 2009 San Francisco Pride parade.

Former Army Lt. Dan Choi was arrested after chaining himself to the White House fence in 2010.

But as a lesbian, she often felt that she was not welcomed by other Asian American or African American liberation activists. "I had not yet come out, and they made it clear that if I did, I would also be out of the liberation community. That threatening message kept me in the closet for the next several years." Helen did come out, and when she married her partner in 2008, they became the first same-sex couple to legally marry in the state of California.

Dan Choi served as a first lieutenant in the army in Iraq, and he seemed to have a bright and shining military career ahead of him. But it was 2008, and the US military still had a repressive policy called "Don't Ask, Don't Tell," which meant that if you were LGBTQIA+, you had to stay closeted and never talk about it. If Dan revealed to anyone that he was gay, his military career would be over. But when he attended the funeral of one of his friends killed in Iraq, Dan decided he couldn't lie any longer. He thought, *When am I going to start living my life?*

Dan came out publicly on a television program in 2009 and was immediately dismissed from military service. He wrote letters to President Barack Obama and joined marches to try to get Don't Ask, Don't Tell repealed. To draw awareness to the issue, Dan handcuffed himself to the White House fence repeatedly over the next year. In 2011, Don't Ask, Don't Tell was repealed. "I can finally say I am not ashamed anymore," Dan wrote. "I joined the military to protect the Constitution. People say it is inappropriate for me to get arrested in uniform, but to me it is the validation of all that I signed up to do."

Even though others had viewed her womanhood and motherhood as a liability, Patsy refused to see herself that way. She put improving the welfare of children at the center of her 1964 campaign for the US House of Representatives. She also proudly ran on her Japanese American heritage and on being a "local girl" who would fight for her neighbors.

Patsy was just as qualified as—even more qualified than— the men she served in Congress with. But the news media seemed obsessed with commenting on her physical appearance. Her Asian heritage, her small frame, and the fact that she was a woman all dominated the news coverage about her. Newspapers would rather write about her outfits than about her accomplishments.

They called her "cute," and said things like, "She has brown eyes, black hair, weighs 110 pounds and is five feet, one and a half inches tall." None of Patsy's male colleagues would have had their dimensions printed in a paper! News articles emphasized how exotic and foreign she was. Most used the term "Oriental" to describe her.

When Patsy first joined Congress, she was one of only thirteen female legislators. The women in Congress had a small fraction of the power, but Patsy was determined to make a difference—especially when it came to discrimination. She knew that meant speaking out, even when it wasn't popular. "It is easy enough to vote right and be consistently with the majority," she said. "But it is more often more important to be ahead of the majority and this means being willing to cut the first furrow in the ground and stand alone for a while if necessary."

Patsy was way ahead of the majority when she helped to champion the passage of a law called Title IX. Pronounced "Title Nine," the law was a seemingly small amendment to a larger education bill. The whole thing is only thirty-seven words long:

From left to right (this page): diver Sammy Lee, the first Asian American male Olympic gold medalist; Vicki Draves, the first Asian American to win Olympic gold; Wataru Misaka, the first non-white player in the NBA; (next page) Mohini Bhardwaj, the first Indian American gymnast to medal in the Olympics; Tiger Woods, of African American and Thai descent, became the youngest professional golfer to achieve a Grand Slam.

No person in the United States shall, on the basis of sex,
be excluded from participation in, be denied the benefits
of, or be subjected to discrimination under any education
program or activity receiving Federal financial assistance.

When President Nixon signed Title IX into law in 1972, it barely
made the newspapers. But those thirty-seven words that Patsy
Mink worked so hard to get passed would transform education
for girls and women.

If you have ever participated in an after-school program, if
you have ever been part of a club or a society at school, then you
have been affected by Title IX. The law states that those school
activities must be equal for all kids, no matter their gender. That's
also true of school admissions, scholarships, and housing. But
the biggest and widest-reaching impact of Title IX has been in
the world of sports.

Because of Title IX, for the first time, schools had to give girls the same opportunities to play sports that boys had. The number of girls playing high school sports exploded from less than 300,000 in 1972 to almost 3.5 million forty-five years later. Sports are more than just games: when you play, you learn teamwork, leadership, confidence, persistence. When girls are treated equally on the playing field, it helps them expect equal treatment everywhere else.

Patsy Mink's tireless work on Title IX helped pave the way for Serena Williams and Megan Rapinoe. And it made it possible for Asian American athletes to become stars: women like snowboarder Chloe Kim, figure skater Michelle Kwan, tennis pro Naomi Osaka, golfer Michelle Wie West, and soccer player Natasha Kai.

Asian American lawmakers like Patsy Mink and Dalip Singh Saund cut a path for future leaders, including Thai American senator Tammy Duckworth, the first woman with a disability elected to Congress, and South Carolina governor Nikki Haley, who was also the first Indian American to serve in a presidential cabinet. In 2021, Kamala Harris made history as the first African American and the first Asian American to hold the office of vice president of the United States.

Patsy Mink's work on Title IX also changed the trajectory for one young girl born in St. Paul, Minnesota, who in 2021 took home the Olympic gold medal in Women's All-Around Gymnastics: Sunisa "Suni" Lee.

When Suni Lee stepped onto the medal podium in Tokyo, she carried the dreams of generations of her people up the steps with her. In addition to being the first Asian American woman to win all-gold, Suni was also the first Hmong American Olympian.

But long before her family celebrated her gold medals, they had been fighting just to survive. Suni's family's story, like the stories of so many Asian Americans who came to this country fleeing the ravages of war, is one of both heartbreak and hope.

SEEKING REFUGE:
SOUTHEAST ASIAN AMERICANS

In the summer of 2021, Suni Lee flipped, swung, and vaulted her way into history. She was already the first Hmong American Olympian, and now she had become the first Hmong American Olympic gold medalist.

All over the world, people marveled at Suni's incredible skills. They also watched videos of her large extended family gathered in her hometown of St. Paul, Minnesota, cheering her on, their faces streaming with tears of pride. That night, their girl was making history for her community and her country. It was a history that stretched from St. Paul all the way across the Pacific Ocean to Southeast Asia. Suni's parents, like 1.2 million Vietnamese, Laotian, Hmong, and Cambodians, had fled to the US as refugees escaping the violence and devastation of the Vietnam War after 1975.

This is the story that begins with the end of one of the longest and most destructive wars on the planet. Today in the United States, we call it the Vietnam War, but in fact, that war engulfed

Sunisa Lee competes in the Women's Uneven Bars Final in the Tokyo 2020 Olympic Games, 2021.

the entire region of Southeast Asia and destroyed lives and land throughout Vietnam, Cambodia, and Laos. The story of that war starts with colonization, with a policy of *Taking and Keeping* that turned half a continent upside down.

War brings suffering, death, and destruction.

For the people of Vietnam—both in the north and in the south—the war meant bombs, bombs, and more bombs. More than a million tons of bombs were dropped on North Vietnam and 4 million were dropped on South Vietnam. The United States also used napalm, an extremely flammable gel that causes so much pain and destruction that its use was later outlawed by the United Nations. The US had intended to use napalm to limit its enemy's ability to arm and supply its troops. But too often, this inhumane weapon was unleashed on civilians.

THE WAR IN VIETNAM

In the late 1800s, when Britain claimed *Takers Keepers* on India, and when the United States claimed *Takers Keepers* on the Philippines, France had claimed ownership over Cambodia, Vietnam, and Laos. They called their new empire "French Indochina." After World War II, when most other Western countries were abandoning their empires in Asia, France had no plans of letting go.

For ten years, France fought against Vietnamese nationalists in what came to be called the First Indochina War. When the war was over, the French abandoned their hopes of retaining their Asian empire. The US worried that they were losing an ally in a region that was so close to Russia and China, the two largest communist nations. The peace agreement divided Vietnam into North (communist) and South (anti-communist), with stipulations that an election would be held to reunite the countries. The election never took place.

The United States, operating under its new policy of using its power to contain the spread of communism, tried to directly determine the fate of Vietnam using military force. 3.4 million American service members were sent overseas to Southeast Asia. Asian Americans who served in the Vietnam War often experienced racism from other soldiers and commanding officers, and were sometimes even mistaken for the enemy by their own comrades.

After over a decade of fighting, more than 58,000 Americans had lost their lives. Facing heavy losses in Vietnam and waning support at home, the US signed a peace treaty in 1973 and began pulling out its troops. In 1975, communist forces seized the southern capital of Saigon and the South Vietnamese government surrendered. A combined 1.3 million Vietnamese soldiers died in the war, and up to 2 million civilians were killed. In the end, America's strategy of "containment" failed, and Vietnam was unified under a communist government.

"I was born in Vietnam into a world at war. Our life was war. We lived and breathed war," one refugee later recalled. Twelve million people in South Vietnam—about half the country's total population—were forced to leave their homes during the war and moved throughout the country in search of safety.

But Vietnam was not the only country affected by this war.

Laos is often skimmed over by history books when discussing the Vietnam War. But the people of Laos were drawn deeply into the conflict, and by the war's end, it had become the most bombed country in the history of human civilization.

Because Vietnam was under such heavy fire, the North Vietnamese began moving their troops and supplies through Laos to reach the fighting in the south. To counter this, the United States needed to get into Laos. But there was a problem.

After the French pulled out of Laos, the country had elected a communist government, which the US was opposed to. The US had agreed to sign a treaty with other nations that they would not interfere in Laos, and Laos would be neutral in the Vietnam War. It was a treaty that the US violated almost immediately. The Central Intelligence Agency (the spy agency of the US, otherwise known as the CIA) began working in secret with a leader inside Laos named Vang Pao. Pao was anti-communist and he was Hmong.

There is no Hmong nation or country. The Hmong are an Indigenous ethnic group who lived in southwestern China for thousands of years. When the Chinese government began pushing them out, some Hmong migrated to the mountains of northern Vietnam, Thailand, Myanmar, and Laos. In the years before the Vietnam

War, the Hmong in Laos had been persecuted by communists, which had turned many of them anti-communist. This meant that their interests and the interests of the US lined up.

Hmong leader Vang Pao made a secret agreement with the US that he would recruit Hmong fighters to help the Americans in the region. In exchange, the US would give the Hmong weapons, training, and humanitarian aid. Some Hmong say that the US even promised that at the war's end, the Hmong people would be given a sanctuary, a protected homeland, where they could finally live in peace. If that's true, then the US never followed through with their promise.

A fifteen-year-old soldier of Vang Pao's secret army (1972). He had been serving since he was thirteen.

But the Hmong? They delivered.

By 1969, Vang Pao commanded a secret army of 40,000 soldiers. They were invaluable to the United States military and were even called "America's most lethal weapon" during the Vietnam War. The Hmong sacrificed everything to help the US. Boys as young as twelve years old were recruited to fight. Hmong soldiers faced heavy casualties. And 50,000 Hmong civilians—one-sixth of the entire population—were killed or wounded during the war.

Laos itself was engulfed in bombs. To target the North Vietnamese who were moving through the Laotian countryside, the US dropped over 2 million tons of explosives. One in four Laotians was uprooted and had to move, many of them moving more than once. This made Laos the country with the most displaced population in the world.

And yet, US actions in Laos and the Hmong army were kept a secret. It wasn't the only secret America was keeping.

The US also dropped over 100,000 tons of bombs on Cambodia, which was in the middle of its own civil war at the time. The bombings were intended to target North Vietnamese troops, and the US military claimed that the bombs were dropped "only in unpopulated parts of Cambodia." But this was not true, and US officials knew it. More innocent Cambodian civilians were killed in these bombings than American military died during the war.

All this destruction had been meant to thwart communist forces in Cambodia. But the bombings actually made some Cambodian people *more* sympathetic to communism. And the bombings also forced the North Vietnamese soldiers deeper into Cambodia, where they were able to help the communist faction called the Khmer Rouge. When the Cambodian civil war came to an end, the Khmer Rouge emerged victorious, and began a reign of fear and genocide.

* * *

When the United States decided to pull out of Vietnam completely in 1975, it was a rushed and chaotic exit. Once US troops and personnel began leaving, the government in South Vietnam started to fall. Vietnamese citizens who had sided with the US feared what might happen to them when the communist government took over. They scrambled to find a way out of the country before everything collapsed.

One Vietnamese woman who had worked for a US oil company did everything she could to get visas and permission to seek asylum in America. When she finally got her paperwork approved, she hurried home and told her family they had two hours to get ready.

Two hours to pack for an unknown journey.

Two hours to figure out what to do about all the thousand details of your life.

Two hours to say goodbye to the ones you are leaving behind, not knowing if you will ever see them again.

They sped to the airport, where thousands of other refugees crowded to leave. They boarded a US military transport plane and eventually made it to Honolulu. By the time they landed, newspapers declared that communist tanks had rolled into the southern capital of Saigon and the South Vietnamese government had surrendered. The family had gotten out just in time. But they realized that they would likely never see their other relatives or their homeland again. "I felt myself falling apart," her son recalled. "My heart had shattered to pieces. I lost not only my country but also everything I had loved."

US planes evacuated 7,500 people a day from Saigon before it fell to the North Vietnamese. Another 73,000 people escaped by sea. In Cambodia, 4,600 people were also evacuated and admitted into the United States. These people made up the "first wave" of refugees from the wars in Southeast Asia. Most of them were diplomats, or educated people with the resources to arrange their own evacuation.

South Vietnamese civilians try to climb the wall of the US Embassy in Saigon on April 29, 1975, in an attempt to flee the country. On the other side, the last American evacuation helicopters were leaving Vietnam.

But there was no large-scale evacuation for the Hmong in Laos. As the communist forces gained power in the country, they violently singled out the Hmong for helping the United States. To be Hmong in Laos was to be a walking target.

Huge crowds of Hmong gathered at the Long Cheng airport, swarming the tarmac, desperate to be airlifted out by US planes. But there were not nearly enough airplanes to hold everyone. Mao Vang Lee, who had worked for the CIA, described the scene: "As soon as the airplane lands, the crowd was already packed underneath it before it came to a halt. They would fight, step on each other to get in the plane."

The US only evacuated 25 percent of the Hmong who came to the airport. When the last US planes took off from the air base, the crew dumped duffel bags full of Laotian money onto the runway as a diversion. Yia Lee, who was one of those left stranded, said, "Everyone cried. In those moments, there was a sense of hopelessness. No dreams for the future. You become like thin air."

Those who were left behind in Laos faced grim choices. The communist forces in Laos were systematically killing all Hmong they could find. Hmong families could either hide in the forest, living in fear in the shadows for the rest of their lives, or they could make the dangerous trek to the border and try to cross the Mekong River into Thailand.

Kao Kalia Yang's family was one of the many who attempted the deadly crossing. Raised in the mountains, most Hmong didn't know how to swim, and many drowned in the swirling currents of the river. Kalia's mother strapped her baby (Kalia's older sister) to her chest. Her father tied her grandmother to his body. Behind them, they could hear the crack of guns. The communist soldiers were coming for them.

They plunged into the cold water. Kalia's father tried his best to swim, pulling his family along. Finally, his feet touched the river bottom on the other side. As he dragged the rest of the family behind him, he saw communist gunboats pulling other Hmong people out of the water to take them back to Laos, where they would likely face execution.

Kalia's family was safe for now. They would eventually walk to a Thai refugee camp, where they would join tens of thousands of other Hmong refugees. Kalia would be born in that camp, within sight, but out of reach, of her ancestors' homeland.

Hmong family in Ban Vinai refugee camp, Thailand, ca. 1978.

Many Hmong languished in the crowded, dirty refugee camps for years before finally being approved to resettle in the United States.

At first, the United States embraced its role as a safe harbor for refugees from Southeast Asia. Over the decades following the Vietnam War, 1.2 million refugees were admitted and resettled in American communities. Public sympathy in America was high for the first arrivals, prompted by the heart-wrenching photographs of fleeing families that filled the front pages of newspapers. There was a collective understanding that the US bore responsibility for upending so many lives through its military action in the Vietnam War. But the wars in Southeast Asia had been like an earthquake. And the aftershocks lasted decades.

The total numbers of refugees driven out of their homelands are so high that it's hard to wrap your head around them. More than 2.5 million Southeast Asian refugees were resettled around the world after the Vietnam War. That's as if nearly every living person in the city of Chicago, Illinois, was forced to leave and find a new home all the way across the globe.

When Kao Kalia Yang was almost seven years old, her family finally received approval to leave the camp and make the journey to their new home in St. Paul, Minnesota.

Like it is for many Hmong families, their arrival was full of both relief and confusion. Few Hmong had any formal education or had even lived in a city before. The culture shock of being plopped into the middle of America was overwhelming. They couldn't communicate with the people around them. They had to figure out how to find food, how to navigate the city streets, and how to take care of themselves and their families.

On top of the shock, refugees were often placed in low-income, urban neighborhoods, mixed in with other minorities who lived in public housing. The language barrier and the lack of skills suitable for city jobs meant that many Hmong were unemployed despite wanting desperately to work. Elderly Hmong, who had once held positions of respect in their communities, found themselves relying on their children more and more. Hmong children were learning English and American customs in school, and they started to carry more responsibility at home. For older Hmong, this was both a blessing and a blow to their dignity. Researchers working with Hmong refugees explained that "it's hard to present yourself as a wise man if your sons or daughters have to teach you how to cross the street or dial the phone."

While Americans had been eager to help the first wave of refugees who arrived in 1975, by the early 1980s, "compassion fatigue" had started to set in. Refugees bore the brunt of anti-Asian and anti-immigrant racism. Some people began to whisper that this was yet another "Asian invasion." One California congressman said, "We already have too many Orientals."

"Next to waves of hello, we received the middle finger," remembers Kao Kalia Yang. People often yelled at her family to "go home."

Home to where, exactly? Historian Chia Vang writes that the Hmong had "been loyal Americans before they even set foot on American soil," and for that loyalty, they could never return to their ancestral homelands, no matter how much they longed for it. The racist taunts were painful to endure. So was the ignorance when Americans didn't know who the Hmong were, or weren't aware that Hmong soldiers had fought fiercely alongside US veterans, saving countless American lives. Had all that sacrifice been for nothing?

Like so many before them, Hmong Americans turned to their own communities for sanctuary and support.

There may be no other place that seems more opposite to the forest-covered mountains of Southeast Asia than urban St. Paul, Minnesota, with its long, harsh winters. But a strong and vibrant Hmong community began to coalesce there. News spread to new Hmong refugees arriving in the US that Minnesota was a nice place to live. There was housing, schools, and jobs. By the 1990s, St. Paul had become the "Hmong capital of the world." Aunties, uncles, friends, and cousins shared information with each other: Which job training programs are the best? Where can you get the best deal on a hundred-pound bag of rice? How can Hmong survive in America?

For Hmong Americans, the struggles they faced because of US-backed wars kept the myth of the model minority out of reach. Hmong Americans have some of the lowest college graduation rates, and the poverty rate among Hmong is almost twice that of the general US population. But those numbers are changing. The poverty rate is declining and the rate of education is growing.

Hmong Americans have worked to tell their own stories and their history of being US allies during the Vietnam War. Hmong veterans proudly wear their military uniforms and medals.

Kao Kalia Yang (right) with her cousins Mai Yia and Dawb in St. Paul, 1987. Kalia wrote of her family's experience escaping Laos, surviving in a refugee camp in Thailand, and eventually moving to the United States.

By building awareness, they pushed Congress to pass the Hmong Veterans' Naturalization Act in 2000, which helped 45,000 people become citizens.

A new generation of Hmong Americans have risen to become leaders in their communities. Kao Kalia Yang became an artist and an author, writing about her family's experiences in books for both adults and children.

In 1992, one newspaper covered six Hmong college graduates in one extended family—the first in their families to attend college. One of those was Mee Moua, who went on to become the first Hmong American elected to state legislature.

When another Hmong American "first," Suni Lee, climbed the steps of the Olympic podium in 2021, media outlets proclaimed her to be an example of the American Dream. It was a complicated turn of phrase, considering that Suni's family would probably not have come to America at all if it hadn't been for an American-led war and a chaotic retreat that forced them to leave the lands of their home. But one thing was certain: that night, when Suni won gold for her country, she also carried the dreams and joys of so many Hmong Americans with her onto the international stage.

"IT'S BECAUSE OF YOU"–
THE MURDER OF VINCENT CHIN

You can tell, just from the warm smile that shines out from his photographs, that Vincent Chin was the kind of person people liked to be around. Vincent ran on the track team. He liked fishing and cars, was a good son to his mother, and had lots of friends in his hometown of Detroit, Michigan.

At twenty-seven years old, Vincent was engaged to a beautiful young woman named Vickie. To save money for their wedding, he worked two jobs: at an engineering firm in the day and waiting tables at a Chinese restaurant at night. He was ambitious and intelligent, a happy person with a bright future ahead of him.

No one who knew Vincent would have ever thought that on a warm summer night in 1982, this all-American kid, beloved by his friends and family, would end up as the victim of a brutal murder, or that the fight for justice over his killing would unite and galvanize Asian Americans all over the country.

Vincent Chin

A week before Vincent and Vickie's wedding, Vincent decided to organize a last-minute bachelor party with his friends at a bar and dance hall. The club was hopping, noisy, and crowded. Among the patrons were forty-two-year-old autoworker Ronald Ebens and his stepson, Michael Nitz. The two white men were there to have a good time, and perhaps forget their troubles for a little while. Like so many in Detroit at the time, Nitz had just lost his job. Over 100,000 autoworkers had been laid off after car production slowed and auto plants around Michigan had closed.

Witnesses later said that Ebens seemed annoyed that Vincent was receiving so much attention from one of the female dancers at the club. He began insulting Vincent, suggesting that he wasn't a real man. Vincent's friends overheard Ebens use the slurs "chink" and "nip" at Vincent.

And then one of the dancers heard Ebens shout in Vincent's direction: "It's because of ****ers like you that we're out of work!"

Vincent stood up to Ebens and shouted at him not to call him those names. What happened in the next few minutes is not exactly clear. Punches were thrown, people were shoved. A chair slammed into Michael Nitz, cutting his forehead. After a few chaotic minutes, the club's security kicked everyone out. The fight should have been over, but it didn't stop there.

Out in the parking lot, Vincent continued shouting at Ebens. Ebens grabbed a baseball bat from the trunk of his car and rushed at Vincent. Vincent ran away, into the night. Ebens and Nitz got in their car and drove around the area, searching. They spotted Vincent sitting on a curb outside a McDonald's restaurant with his friend.

Ebens got out of the car and charged at a shocked Vincent with the baseball bat. Nitz grabbed on to Vincent so he couldn't get away, and Ebens slammed the bat into Vincent's shoulder. Ebens swung the bat into Vincent again. And again. He hit Vincent in the head with the bat "as if he were going for a home run," said one witness.

Two off-duty police officers stopped Ebens at gunpoint.

But it was too late.

Vincent Chin died from his injuries four days later. For his mother, fiancée, friends, and community, the loss was almost too much to bear. And then came the news about his killers.

Instead of facing murder charges, Ebens and Nitz pleaded guilty to manslaughter. There is a big difference between the two. Manslaughter is when someone kills another person without forethought, "in the heat of the moment." Murder is intentional and planned. The police officer who had witnessed the attack on Vincent was shocked to learn about their plea. To him, it seemed like Ebens and Nitz had time to cool off after the fight at the club. They had time to think about what they were going to do to Vincent.

The manslaughter plea meant that Ebens and Nitz would not face a trial with a jury but would be sentenced by a judge. The judge's verdict?

A $3,000 fine and probation.

That was all.

The Asian American community of Detroit was outraged. *This* was justice?

"You go to jail for killing a dog," said a local restaurant owner. "Vincent's life was worth less than a used car," said a family friend.

Journalist Helen Zia and lawyer Liza Chan, who investigated the case, noted that there had been mistakes made by the justice system all along the way. The police didn't interview key witnesses, and the court records were sloppy and incomplete.

But even more obvious to everyone was that the main reason there had not been justice for Vincent Chin had to do with his race and the race of his killers. The judge who handed down the light sentence for Ebens and Nitz had said, "They weren't the kind of people you sent to prison. I just didn't think putting them in prison would do any good for them or for society. You don't make the punishment fit the crime; you make the punishment fit the criminal."

But that's not how it's supposed to work.

Basically, the judge was saying that he was swayed by *who* the killers were and not the brutality of *what* they had done.

For Vincent's Asian American community, the words that Ebens had shouted during their fight said it all: "It's because of you." For them, the writing on the wall was clear.

Vincent had been killed because he was Asian American.

They knew all too well what had motivated his killers because they had experienced the same hatred in their own lives.

By the early 1980s, Detroit had fallen on hard times. The city had once been a booming industrial hub of the Midwest, with good jobs and lots of economic growth. But after protests against racial segregation and discrimination led to multiday riots in 1967, hundreds of thousands of white residents moved out, turning neighborhoods into ghost towns. The 1970s had seen an oil crisis and a recession that only increased the poverty and housing troubles in the city.

While American auto companies continued to churn out heavy, clunky cars that required a lot of gas to run, Japanese car companies were investing in new technologies and producing light, inexpensive cars. The American auto industry was losing sales fast to its Japanese competitors, and that meant they had to close factories and lay off thousands of workers to stay afloat.

These had been good, reliable jobs that had paid a high salary. Autoworkers had been able to buy homes, send their kids to college, and invest in their future. And then suddenly, all that vanished.

But rather than blame the American auto executives for their poor planning and decision-making, most autoworkers blamed the Japanese competition.

If this sounds like a familiar storyline, it's because it is. Once again, Asian Americans were taking the fall for the actions and policies of others.

Old hatreds and fears began bubbling back up again. One bumper sticker of the time said, "Datsun, Toyota, Nissan. Remember Pearl Harbor!" One Japanese American woman recalled a colleague telling her, "Why don't you go back to Japan with the cars."

The news media and politicians fanned the flames of racial hatred. As they had during World War II, lawmakers saw an opportunity to gain votes by promising to punish the "foreigners" who were taking jobs away from Americans. One Michigan politician referred to the Japanese car companies as "the little yellow people." Another said, "If I were president . . . I'd fix the Japanese like they have never been fixed." And the chairman of the Chrysler automotive company casually said the US should drop more nuclear weapons on Japan.

Politicians may have downplayed their remarks as "just words." But words can be dangerous. And when politicians—people who are supposed to be our leaders—use them, it gives those dangerous words even more power.

According to journalist Helen Zia, "It felt dangerous to have an Asian face. Asian American employees of auto companies were warned not to go onto the factory floor because angry workers might hurt them if they were thought to be Japanese."

And so those words—"it's because of you"—had sent a chill through many Asian Americans in Detroit and all over the country.

It didn't matter if they were of Chinese or Japanese descent or not. Asian Americans knew what it felt like to be targeted and threatened just because of the way they looked. They saw themselves in Vincent Chin.

It was the voice of Vincent's mother, Lily, that first called out for justice. Vincent's father had fought in the US Army during World War II, and he brought Lily to America from her hometown in Kaiping, China, after the war. Unable to have their own children, the Chins decided to adopt a child from their home region of China. The adoption process took years, and when Vincent finally stepped off the plane in America, he was six years old. Right away, he became his mother's whole world. Lily had been so happy about his upcoming wedding. She dreamed of grandchildren one day. After losing her only child, she had to do something.

And so, just as Mary Tape had written a letter one hundred years earlier to stand up for equal rights for her daughter, Lily Chin wrote a letter demanding equal justice for her son. She sent her letter to the Detroit Chinese Welfare Council. This letter was the spark the movement needed to catch fire.

In May 1983, a group of hundreds of protestors gathered in downtown Detroit, calling for a federal investigation into Vincent's murder. The Chinese community was the first to organize, but they were also joined by Japanese Americans, Korean Americans, Filipino Americans, and African Americans. Local churches, synagogues, the NAACP, and the Detroit Association of Black

Organizations called for justice alongside Asian Americans. The group of multiracial protesters called themselves American Citizens for Justice (ACJ). They wanted everyone to know that Vincent's killing had been racially motivated. But they knew they would have a tough time convincing other Americans that the so-called model minority could be victims of racist hate crimes, too.

Supporters across the country held their own rallies to cry out for justice. The protests drew the attention of the media. It was rare to see big crowds of Asian Americans, African Americans, and others gathering and demanding action together. Detroit's Asian American community had started a new civil rights movement that had spread throughout the nation.

Protestors march in a Justice for Vincent Chin rally in Detroit, 1983.

Despite the public pressure, the judge who let Ebens and Nitz go free refused to change his original sentence, saying, "If it had been a brutal murder" then he would have sent them to prison. Vincent's friends were appalled. How much more brutal did a killing have to be for an Asian American to get justice?

But something had changed. Asian Americans all over the country refused to be silenced. Rallies for Vincent Chin swelled to over 500 people. Lily Chin continued to press for justice for her son in the media and by visiting lawmakers in Washington, DC. The ACJ, with the leadership of Helen Zia and Liza Chan, wanted to bring a federal civil rights investigation of the case, but they faced an uphill battle. Even some law professors didn't believe that the current civil rights laws in America applied to Asians or non-Black Americans. Race in America was still seen by many as a white or Black issue.

In fact, when the police filled out the report the night of Vincent's murder, there were only two choices to mark the victim's race: white or black. Vincent had been categorized as white.

Helen Zia pointed out how harmful the model minority myth was in this case. "The stereotype that Asians in America are not targets of racial violence certainly played a significant role in Vincent Chin's case and the fact that a judge and jury allowed his killers to go free."

In 1984, the federal civil rights case against the two men found Ebens guilty and sentenced him to twenty-five years in prison. Nitz was found not guilty. Ebens later appealed and a jury in Ohio cleared him of all charges. The result was heartbreaking. After all the evidence, after all the public outcry for justice, Vincent's killers would not spend a single full day in jail. Later, a civil suit was filed, and Ebens was ordered to pay the Chin family $1.5 million dollars, spread out in payments for the rest of his life. He never paid any of it.

Not that any amount of money could bring Vincent back. Nor could it erase the lack of justice for Vincent's loved ones.

And yet, the fight for Vincent Chin had not been in vain. The court cases had built public awareness of the racism and discrimination faced by Asian Americans. And the Asian American community had come together in a new and important way.

Chinese American lawyer Frank H. Wu has said, "If you talk to Asian Americans who came of age back then and became journalists or lawyers or who stood up and spoke out, so many of them will tell you it's because of the Vincent Chin case. It's that case that made me do what I do. That case changed my life."

Important Asian American and civil rights organizations like the Asian Pacific American Legal Resource Center and the Asian Law Caucus came together and formed the National APA Legal Consortium in 1991. They would continue to work to ensure that victims of hate crimes could get justice.

And the unfairness exposed through Vincent's case would spark efforts to improve the legal system for all Americans. On the day that Ebens's first sentence was handed out, no one had told Vincent's family, and so his mother had not even been present at the courthouse. If she had known, she would have been there.

Because of Vincent's case, Congress passed the Victims of Crime Act, which ensured that victims or their families could have their statements read as part of court proceedings.

Today, what happened to Vincent would be classified as a hate crime. In part because of the spotlight that Vincent's case shone on the justice system, there is now a federal hate crime law that protects people from being targeted because of their race, religion, ethnicity, nationality, gender, sexual orientation, gender identity, or disability.

The fight for justice for Vincent Chin also brought Asian Americans together in a new and lasting way. For many, Vincent's killing was on the extreme end of the spectrum of discrimination they faced in their everyday lives.

For Hmong American Mee Moua, seeing Asian Americans of so many different backgrounds marching together under one cause was electrifying. "My experience as a Hmong refugee was connected to the experience of other Asian Americans," she said. Moua went on to become an activist fighting with others to create a more equitable society for all.

The rallies for Vincent Chin showed Mee that when Asian Americans called out for justice and joined alongside other racial groups, they could create real change in this country.

LEFT TO BURN:
KOREATOWN ON SA I GU

Eleven-year-old Kat Kim was confused.

Every morning her mom woke up very early to open their family restaurant for the day. But as the hours went by on the morning of April 30, 1992, her mother still hadn't gone into work. Kat watched television as she waited. The news programs showed footage of a crowd gathered around a courthouse. They cut to film of people beating up cars, and other footage of different people breaking the windows of police cars. It was her local Los Angeles news station, but the violence seemed far away.

Finally, Kat's mom came out of her room and said that they were going to the restaurant, and that they would need Kat's help. At the restaurant, she expected to be told to start setting tables. Instead, her mother was grabbing what she could out of the cash register and loading equipment from the storage room into the back of the car.

Next door, the owners of the liquor store had asked Kat's mom for paper place mats. They were taping them over the window, trying to hide the signs that said it was a liquor store. *What's going on?* Kat wondered. No one would explain it to her.

When they got back home, Kat returned to watching television. The news footage now showed people breaking into stores and *looting*—taking what they wanted without paying. They were smashing windows and taking everything from inside: televisions, shoes, groceries, all sorts of things. Suddenly, Kat recognized one of the stores being looted. It was just down the block from her parents' restaurant. Now she understood. The violence was not far away. The violence was right here, in Koreatown.

Businesses continue to burn out of control on Vermont Avenue as seen in the north direction at San Marino Street in Koreatown, Los Angeles, California, on May 1, 1992, during the third day of the 1992 Los Angeles riots.

Kat's neighborhood of Koreatown was like a miniature Korea right in the middle of Los Angeles. There were so many Korean immigrants gathered in one neighborhood that you could go the whole day eating Korean food, shopping at Korean stores, attending Korean church, and hearing only Korean spoken. Many Korean Americans were subjected to racism and discrimination outside Koreatown, so this neighborhood felt like a safe and welcoming place.

Most Korean Americans had immigrated to the area recently, in the years since the 1965 Immigration Act had passed. For many of them, the model minority myth didn't apply. They were a highly educated group, but almost 40 percent spoke little to no English, and 14 percent lived below the poverty line. As they worked to establish themselves in America, Korean Americans looked for affordable areas of town where they could buy homes and start their own businesses. They began to push outside the bounds of Koreatown, into neighborhoods that had traditionally been African American and Hispanic.

For African American Los Angelenos, decades of racist housing laws and discrimination had meant that they had never been allowed to fully integrate into the city. In many ways, the African American community was similar to an immigrant community because of how they had been kept on the margins. By the 1990s, decades of oppression had taken a toll.

The neighborhood that had once been a good, safe place for African Americans to raise their families was changing. Similar to the way that American car companies in Detroit had shut down and laid off workers, employers had left south central Los Angeles, taking the good jobs with them. They left their trash behind in their abandoned factories. And the city did little to stop it, or to invest in other industries that could provide jobs.

Crime began going up. Families who could afford it moved out. They sold their businesses. Liquor stores sold their liquor licenses. They found willing buyers in the new Korean immigrants who were moving to the area. By the late 1980s, close to 70 percent of the businesses in south central LA were owned by Korean Americans.

These recent Korean immigrants had missed the civil rights movement of the 1960s, and many were unaware of the struggles and sacrifices African Americans had made. They didn't know that the very law that had made it possible for so many Asian Americans to immigrate to the US might never have happened if African Americans hadn't fought for equality. While some Korean Americans sympathized with their African American neighbors, others adopted racist, anti-Black views.

Newspapers began to run stories about Koreatown that focused on the "Black-Korean conflict." In these stories, the focus was on crimes committed by African American people and the rude, racist Korean shop owners. But this was just a fraction of the full story.

The papers never reported on the economy or how the government had failed this area. The articles didn't try to pick apart how decades of oppressive laws had created these tensions. They didn't interview the diverse people of the neighborhoods, leaving out the growing Latine community altogether. And they didn't cover the local groups of Korean, African American, and other citizens who had been working together to bridge divides and heal their communities.

Maybe the writers didn't think those kinds of stories would sell as many newspapers. Maybe it was simpler to slice off a fraction of the story and pretend that it was the whole thing. Simpler than tackling hundreds of years of social and racial injustice.

This kind of simple storytelling by the media and by politicians would continue, and it would get worse in the years leading up to March of 1991, when a girl named Latasha Harlins walked into a liquor store in Koreatown.

The liquor stores in Koreatown sold more than just liquor. They offered drinks, snacks, household items, and for some low-income families, they were the only places in their neighborhoods to buy groceries. In March of 1991, fifteen-year-old Latasha Harlins picked up a bottle of orange juice in a Koreatown liquor store. The Korean American store owner accused her of trying to steal it. They argued. The owner grabbed Latasha's backpack. Latasha struck the owner with her fist. She left the orange juice behind and started to walk out the door. And then the store owner picked up her gun from behind the counter and shot Latasha in the back of the head, killing her instantly.

At the trial that November, the jury convicted the store owner of manslaughter. The judge in the case sentenced her to probation and a $500 fine. In April of 1992, an appeals court upheld the judge's decision. No jail time for the killer of this fifteen-year-old girl.

If this sounds chillingly similar to Vincent Chin's case, it's because it was. But this time, a security camera had captured footage of the entire incident. It was clear to anyone watching the tape that Latasha had not been a threat when the store owner had shot her from behind. Just like there had been no justice for Vincent Chin in 1982, one decade later, there would be no justice for Latasha Harlins.

Shortly afterward, the verdict in the Rodney King case was announced.

Around the same time that the killing of Latasha Harlins had been caught on security cameras, the brutal beating of an African American man by police officers had been recorded on video. Rodney King had been pulled over by the Los Angeles police for drunk driving. A bystander captured video footage of the unarmed, cooperative King being viciously and repeatedly beaten by four police officers with batons. The video was sent to local TV stations and replayed on the news all over the country.

With that video evidence, it seemed that finally, *finally* the rest of the world was going to see what African American Los Angelenos had to endure from the police on a regular basis. But then the jury announced their decision on the fate of the police officers who had beaten Rodney King nearly to death—

—not guilty.

It was too much. Heartache, despair, anger, frustration, exhaustion. For some African Americans, all these emotions and more boiled over. In a 1967 speech, Dr. Martin Luther King, Jr., said that "a riot is the language of the unheard." African Americans living in Los Angeles had been crying out for justice and equality for decades. If Americans could watch footage of Latasha Harlins and Rodney King and *still* not listen to the truth, then what would get their attention?

The Rodney King verdict was a tipping point. A match thrown onto kindling. And the ensuing flames would engulf Koreatown.

People join hands holding up a water hose to put out fires at a shopping center at the intersection of Western Avenue and Sixth Street, as LA city firefighters were not able to respond to the fire during the 1992 Los Angeles riots.

For five days, the city of Los Angeles erupted into chaos. Looting, arson, and destruction. At one point, there were nineteen simultaneous fires burning in the city. As the riots continued, it became clear that some areas of town would be protected from rioters by police while others would not. The fire department said they could not safely deploy to some areas, and so those parts of the city burned.

Koreatown was one of the neighborhoods where the citizens were on their own.

Korean American leaders got on Korean-language radio and called for people to show up at stores and restaurants and bring whatever firearms they owned. These businesses were all that these families had. If they were going to save them from destruction, they would have to do it themselves.

Kat Kim's uncle gathered his friends at his car dealership. He distributed guns and instructed them to guard the property. It was the first time Kat had ever heard of someone using a gun outside of the movies. Asian Americans owned guns? Kat didn't even understand where they would have gotten them.

Many of the Korean American men were first-generation immigrants who had served in the military back in Korea, where service was mandatory. They owned their own firearms, and they knew how to use them. They set up sandbags and makeshift barricades outside their stores and posted armed sentries on the rooftops.

Streetlights and traffic lights were out. Windows were smashed.

Cars were on fire. *Everything* seemed to be burning. There was no sign of the police anywhere.

It was like a war zone. A war zone in the center of one of America's largest and most prosperous cities. For the Korean and African American organizers who had been trying for years to build solidarity and trust in their communities, their dreams of interracial cooperation seemed to be going up in smoke.

By the time the National Guard was finally called out and the rioting ceased, sixty-three people had lost their lives. Property damages were estimated at $1 billion. For the Korean American immigrants whose businesses had been looted, they lost everything they had. Many of them would never reopen.

Korean Americans called it "Sa I Gu," or 4-29 in Korean, the date of the first night of the riots, and it became a trauma that followed them like a shadow. The shadow felt colder because people didn't want to talk about it. And few outsiders seemed to understand what had really happened beyond that tiny fraction of the story the news media told.

In 1992, Korean American Grace Lee had just finished college and was visiting relatives abroad in Korea. One night, a relative turned on the TV to a news program that showed footage of Koreatown burning. "I had never seen Koreans on TV before," said Grace. "All of a sudden I'm seeing Korean men with their guns and Korean people weeping in front of their burned-down stores."

The news media kept calling it a "Black riot," a term that didn't sit right with Grace. The footage she saw of African American looters and gun-wielding Koreans didn't fit with the Koreatown she knew. Grace knew it as a diverse and complex place, with Hispanic families, a "Little Bangladesh," an Islamic center. It was a special place where immigrants lived, supported each other, and, yes—a place where conflicts did arise.

She decided to tell her own story about the Koreatown riots by making a documentary film.

To watch Grace's film, you can't just sit back and push play. The film is meant to be viewed online, in an interactive way. As you watch an interview with one person, footage of a different person or a different scene during the riots begins to roll at the same time. The documentary contains almost two thousand interviews. It's a little confusing to watch at times, and you have to pause and go back to catch everything. But you quickly realize that this may be the only way to wrap your head around what happened during those five days. There is no one neat and tidy story of Sa I Gu. To understand, you have to sit in a cloud of stories, voices, and perspectives.

In the days after the riots, Kat Kim drove through Koreatown with her parents. There was an eerie stillness in the air as they passed the burned shells of businesses of their friends and neighbors. There was anger and pain in the Korean community and in the African American community. And distrust on all sides. How were all these people going to keep living together in the same neighborhood after what had just happened?

Kat learned that there was a demonstration being planned for the next week. She was nervous. What would happen? What would it be like?

Thirty thousand people came out for the peaceful march. The crowd was diverse: African Americans, Latines, Koreans, and whites walking together through the street and gathering in a large park. There, leaders took to the microphone, saying that they must not let the riots define who they were as a community. They recognized that it was going to take a lot of work to rebuild their neighborhood, and even more work to build trust between neighbors. Together they called for justice, equality, freedom, and *peace*.

Koreatown March for Peace, May 1992.

In many ways, 1992 was a turning point not just for Korean Americans, but for all Asian Americans. It was a wake-up call that Asian Americans could not turn inward if they wanted to move forward. It was also a reminder that just because Asian Americans were being called the model minority and their status in America was seemingly starting to improve, they still had a choice. They could either stand on the side of the oppressive system that had kept minorities down for centuries, or they could stand with justice and equality. But they could not simply stand aside.

"LOOKING LIKE THE ENEMY"

Simran Jeet Singh and his brothers were typical all-American kids: playing basketball and soccer, studying for their classes, and staying busy with clubs and activities at their school in San Antonio, Texas. They were natural athletes with lots of friends. Not everything was easy for them, though. When Simran was just eleven years old, he was called a terrorist for the first time.

As a Sikh, part of Simran's faith is to wear a turban. This very visible symbol of being Sikh means that sometimes he stands out when he's in a group of people. When he was eleven, during the equipment check before the start of one of his soccer games, the referee demanded to pat down his turban. "Hey, little terrorist!" the ref said to him. "You're not hiding bombs or knives in there, are you?"

Simran was so angry. The racist slur of "terrorist" has long been hurled at Americans with Middle Eastern, Arab, and South Asian heritage, and it is used to especially denigrate Muslims. Simran is Sikh, not Muslim, but when the ref saw Simran's turban and brown skin, he made ignorant assumptions and racist judgments, and he made Simran the target for his cruelty.

And now this referee was going to put his hands all over Simran's turban? It was offensive and degrading. But Simran allowed it. What else could he do? If he didn't, he wouldn't have been able to play with his team. Later, he was mad at himself for giving in and not saying anything about the ref's racism. It was hard to figure out how to respond in a moment like that. Should he refuse? Should he fight? Should he say something mean back? What was the right thing to do?

Simran Jeet Singh in middle school in San Antonio, Texas.

Incidents like that would continue for Simran and his brothers as they grew up, but it didn't define their childhoods. It was true that they practiced a different faith than many of their classmates, but this didn't stop them from having awesome friendships, excelling in school, or feeling safe and happy at home.

Those feelings of love, safety, and belonging would prove vital in just a few short years, when Simran, along with many South Asian, Muslim, and Arab Americans all over the country, would be the targets of intensifying racism and hatred.

On the morning of September 11, 2001, nineteen terrorists hijacked four commercial airplanes from Logan Airport in Boston, Dulles Airport in Washington, DC, and Newark Airport in New Jersey. Three of the planes were intentionally crashed into the North and South Towers of the World Trade Center in New York City and into the Pentagon building in Washington, DC. The fourth plane crashed in a field in Pennsylvania after passengers rushed the cockpit in an attempt to retake the plane and divert it from its suspected target in Washington, DC. The attacks killed almost 3,000 people and were the deadliest terrorist attack in history.

The terrorists were members of Al-Qaeda, an extremist organization primarily located in Afghanistan. Al-Qaeda and other groups that use violence to inflict terror do not represent the 1.8 billion Muslims living in the world today. But the September 11 (9/11) attacks reinforced prejudices and stereotypes about Muslims—and those assumed of being Muslim—that stretch back centuries.

A LONG HISTORY OF ANTI-MUSLIM PREJUDICE

You can trace the West's treatment of Muslims back to the Middle Ages, when European countries waged the Christian Crusades, which were a series of violent religious wars started by Pope Urban II to recapture the Holy Land from the Turks. Pope Urban called on all Christians to go to war—not just on specific Muslim countries but on all Muslim people. The religious intolerance that followed led to the widespread massacre of Muslims, Jews, and other non-Christians.

The Crusades set in motion the idea that Christians and Muslims were opposites and natural enemies. In the travel writings of the nineteenth century, the Middle East was portrayed as an exotic place: full of riches, but also ruled by barbaric people. Just as all Asians had been lumped together in a group of faceless "Orientals," people who had anything that identified them as Middle Eastern,

After the 1965 Immigration Act, South Asian immigrants came with professional skills and college degrees and flourished.

But 9/11 would show just how quickly some Asian Americans could go from the model minority to being labeled a terrorist threat.

Weeks after the September 11 terrorist attacks, nine-year-old Shahana Hanif and her little sister, daughters of Bangladeshi Muslim immigrants, were walking to their local mosque from their home in Brooklyn, New York. As a car passed by them, the driver rolled down his window and yelled at them: "Terrorist!"

Arab, or Muslim would be lumped together in a racial group that was labeled foreign, savage, and violent.

Those people are inferior.

Those people are dangerous.

The reality is that it's impossible to tell what a Muslim person *looks* like, because Islam is a faith, not a race. Yes, there are countries where most of the population practices Islam. But in America, Muslims are among the most racially diverse religious groups in the country.

Muslims had been living in the United States before it was even a nation. An estimated 10 to 15 percent of all enslaved Africans in the US were Muslim, and today, African Americans make up the largest percentage of practicing Muslims in the US. Muslim Americans have fought in every American war since the War of 1812. And some Asian American Muslims can trace their roots to the global mass migrations of the early 1900s that brought family members to the United States to work as farmers, salespeople, and factory workers. Today, 6 to 7 million Americans declare Islam as their faith.

The girls ran, scared and confused. Later, Shahana would struggle to understand—how could anyone look at two little girls wearing hijabs and think they were a threat?

Almost instantly after 9/11, Muslim, Sikh, Hindu, and Arab Americans were being beaten, chased, shot, and stabbed in cities and towns across the nation. Muslim Americans and those who were mistaken for being Muslim were targeted, intimidated, and attacked—even by their own government. In the same way that Japanese Americans were detained and arrested following the bombing of Pearl Harbor, in the days following 9/11, 1,200

Muslim men were labeled as suspicious and detained by US law enforcement.

These targeted campaigns sent the message that the US government believed all Muslims in the US might be dangerous terrorists. And just as it had in the past when our government gave legitimacy to racist or xenophobic fears, violence would follow.

In 2001, Valarie Kaur was a junior at Stanford University when she watched the second plane explode into the South Tower of the World Trade Center. She and her father were still trying to make sense of the enormous tragedy unfolding on their television screen when the news started playing and replaying photos of the person responsible for the attacks: Al-Qaeda's Osama bin Laden, who had brown skin, a black beard, and wore a turban. Valarie had the chilling realization that many Americans would think that "our nation's new enemy looked like my family."

Just days after the attack on the Twin Towers, the phone at Valarie's home in California rang. A family friend in Phoenix called with the news that another close friend—whom Valarie called Balbir Uncle—had been killed. Balbir Singh Sodhi, a Sikh American gas station owner in Arizona, was planting flowers in front of his business when a gunman shot him five times in the back. As they arrested the murderer, he shouted, "I am a patriot!" and "I stand for America, all the way!"

Valarie's uncle Balbir was the first of nineteen people killed in hate crimes in the days and weeks after 9/11. In Texas, a Pakistani-born grocer was killed. In Los Angeles, an Egyptian-born merchant was killed. Mosques were attacked and businesses were vandalized. Anti-Muslim hate crimes grew by 1,600 percent. This hatred and violence targeted many others as well.

Balbir Singh Sodhi was Sikh, not Muslim. But because men who practice the Sikh faith wear turbans and have beards, they have been particularly targeted by ignorant and hateful people. In 2012, seven Sikh Americans were senselessly killed by a white supremacist in a mass shooting at their temple in Oak Creek, Wisconsin. Even decades after 9/11, Sikhs continue to be singled out for racial violence, the victims of more than half of all attacks on South Asians in the US.

Family visiting the memorial honoring Balbir Singh Sodhi outside his gas station in Mesa, Arizona, September 19, 2001.

* * *

For Valarie and other Sikh Americans, the violence they endured after 9/11 was not new. It wasn't new for Muslim Americans, either. But it intensified, fueled by the misconceptions and lack of understanding that most Americans had of both faiths.

In the 1980s and 1990s, American movies and television reinforced the stereotype that Arabs and Muslims were bloodthirsty and violent. For those who have never interacted with Muslim neighbors or friends, much of their information comes from what they see on-screen. These stereotypes portrayed over and over again can be harmful and long-lasting.

Those people are dangerous.

As negative views about Muslim Americans became more common in movies and on the news, Islamophobia (fear of those who practice Islam) became a regular feature in politics. Just as politicians during World War II stoked anti-Japanese fears to get themselves elected, those running for office in the years following 9/11 saw the opportunity to take advantage of Americans' fear and ignorance of Islam.

In 2008, when Barack Obama was first running for president, his political opponents zeroed in on his foreign-sounding name, his Muslim father, and the fact that as a child he had lived in Indonesia (a majority-Muslim nation). Even though Obama is a practicing Christian, politicians and right-wing news outlets openly sowed doubts as to whether he was in fact a Muslim. Giving him that label was also a convenient way to put him down as being "un-American" without calling out his Blackness.

During the 2016 presidential race, Donald Trump put

anti-immigrant, anti-Muslim views at the center of his campaign. In 2015, one year before the election, Trump called for a "total and complete shutdown of Muslims." That year, there was a spike in anti-Muslim hate crimes, the highest number reported since 2001.

Once in office, President Trump made good on his promise to single out Muslims with an executive order that banned anyone from seven countries with majority-Muslim populations from coming to the US. The "Muslim ban," as it came to be known, was challenged immediately in several courts for being unconstitutional.

Many Asian Americans were astounded. History was repeating itself. How was this ban, which singled out travelers based on religion, any different from the Chinese Exclusion Act, which had singled out immigrants based on their race? Hadn't America been through all this before when it had incarcerated 120,000 innocent Japanese Americans?

And yet, in 2018, the Supreme Court allowed Trump's executive order to stand on the grounds that the ban was designed to protect the national security of the United States.

Wait. *Say that again?*

It was the same line of reasoning given when the Supreme Court ruled against Fred Korematsu in 1944. In that year, the court had stated that it was acceptable to imprison an entire race of Americans because it was a "military necessity." How could the Supreme Court be making the same mistake *again*? Especially when the court had acknowledged that the Fred Korematsu decision had been a colossal and shameful mistake.

In fact, the US Justice Department had issued a formal "confession of error" in the Korematsu case. They acknowledged that back in 1944, government lawyers had misled the Supreme Court about the security threat of Japanese Americans. Declassified military documents showed that the US government had incarcerated them not because of any evidence of spying or sabotage but to "boost public morale."

In other words, during World War II, politicians had wanted to be seen as taking action so that Americans could "feel safe," and Japanese Americans had paid dearly for it. With the Muslim ban, the Trump administration was doing the same thing, and it was Muslim Americans paying the price.

Fred Korematsu's daughter, Karen, was livid. In an interview, she argued that the Supreme Court was repeating "the same bad logic of the 1940s decision" and condemned the court for merely replacing "one injustice with another."

Karen Korematsu speaks out against the Trump administration's travel ban against Muslims on the steps of the US Supreme Court, 2018.

In the days after 9/11, Simran's family had received anonymous death threats. People called their house, shouting slurs and curse words. Some strangers even drove by their home, harassing them. But Simran also remembers that even more people checked in on them. Their neighbors, friends, and teammates stopped by the house to bring food and flowers. They wanted the Singh family to know that they had the love and support of their community. "I'll always remember my parents pointing out then, in that moment of extreme difficulty, how one finds hope in the face of adversity: Notice how much more love there is in the world than hate."

In 2017, hours after the Trump administration's Muslim ban went into effect, protests ignited in cities across America. Crowds of thousands of people from many faiths and cultures gathered at the nation's biggest airports. They held signs saying "Let them in," "Welcome Muslims," and "Refugees Welcome."

Demonstrators outside JFK International Airport in New York City in 2017 protest President Donald Trump's ban on Muslim travelers.

Muslim American teens have spoken out against the anti-Muslim backlash that erupted after 9/11 and in the decades since. They have organized to advocate for their own civil rights and to encourage others to get more involved in the political process.

A few days after nine-year-old Shahana Hanif was called a "terrorist" for wearing her hijab in public, she organized a meeting with her sisters and friends in the basement of her Brooklyn home. She drafted a letter to then-president George W. Bush, calling on him to send a message to the American people that the way Muslims were being treated was not acceptable. The president never did write back to her, but the experience of growing up in the shadow of 9/11 kindled a spark in Shahana to stand up for the rights of all Americans. "We needed to grow up in a way to become the warriors of our communities." Two decades later, she would run for public office and win—becoming the first Muslim woman on the New York City Council.

In the decades since 9/11, Sikh Americans continue to get harassed and attacked for being "Muslim" or "terrorists." But many in the Sikh community took collective action: they decided that they would not respond to this ignorance by saying, "I'm not a Muslim." Because saying that might defend themselves against violence, but it would send the message that it was okay to attack actual Muslim Americans. To fight the hatred that was harming Sikh Americans, they would stand in solidarity with Muslim Americans.

During difficult moments, Simran Jeet Singh would find comfort by thinking of how other Sikhs throughout history had shown strength and resilience when persecuted. "The trick is to recognize [the past and present] are intertwined," Simran writes in his memoir, *The Light We Give.* "The past resides within us in each moment because the past shapes each moment and shapes us all, individually and collectively. None of us lives outside history, and none of us lives beyond the present."

ASIAN AMERICAN RECKONINGS

There is a saying: "History repeats itself."

But that lets human beings off too easy.

We make history every day. History is made out of the actions we take and the words we say in the present moment.

In the spring of 2020, the COVID-19 virus was sweeping through the United States. Millions were hospitalized, and within two years, 1 million Americans had died from the disease. Schools and businesses closed, and the economy slowed.

Because the first emergence of the virus had been recorded in China, a conspiracy emerged that the disease had been intentionally imported from China. Some lawmakers and members of the media urged Americans to blame Chinese people for the virus. Instead of using the scientific name for the disease, they used racist language, calling it the "Chinese virus," the "Wuhan virus," and even "kung flu." US senator John Cornyn from Texas told a reporter that "China is to blame because the culture where people eat bats and snakes . . . and things like that."

Just as they had been blamed in the past for lost jobs, low wages, shuttered auto factories, and war, Asian Americans were now being blamed for a global pandemic, even as they also suffered from the losses wrought by COVID-19. The way some public figures tied the COVID-19 virus to Asian Americans and to immigrants was eerily similar to how the Chinese had been blamed for the spread of bubonic plague and other diseases over a century earlier.

In San Francisco, Asian Americans made up 38 percent of all COVID-19 deaths, the most of any ethnicity. Nearly a third of the nurses who died of COVID-19 in the US were Filipino American, even though they made up just 4 percent of the nursing population.

President Donald Trump was very clear that he placed the blame for the COVID-19 pandemic on the Chinese. He repeatedly used racist terms at rallies, during press conferences, during presidential debates, and even at the United Nations. The fact that other Americans would embrace and repeat Trump's anti-Asian messaging (and his anti-immigrant and anti-Muslim language) served as a cruel reminder that even though Asian Americans have a long history and deep roots in this country, they are still viewed as outsiders and foreigners—especially during crises.

When Trump posted on Twitter about the "Chinese virus," his post was shared millions of times. This was the president of the United States of America, the holder of the highest office in the land. History has shown that when elected leaders use racist language, they have the power to fan the flames of hatred and give cover to the racism of others. As could be expected, Trump's remarks track directly with a rise in racist incidents against Asian Americans.

It was in this climate of blame that six Korean American women were murdered in Atlanta, Georgia. It was in this climate of hatred that the elderly, like eighty-four-year-old Thai American Vicha Ratanapakdee, were callously attacked and killed. It was in this climate of ignorance that Sikh Americans at a warehouse in Indianapolis, Indiana, were targeted and massacred.

The rise in violence was a wake-up call for America. Anti-Asian hate crimes were up 339 percent between 2020 and 2021. The numbers took many by surprise. The model minority myth had been used effectively, not just to push back against calls for racial justice for African Americans but also to make all racism in the US feel like a thing of the past.

The day after the murders at the spa in Atlanta, President Joe Biden said, "The recent attacks against the [Asian American] community are un-American. They must stop." The president had meant to be sympathetic, but his comment was simply not true. Anti-Asian American racism *has* been a part of the nation's history for centuries.

Because the history of Asian Americans has been ignored or forgotten, stereotypes have flourished. Asian Americans have been painted as forever foreigners, exotic objects of desire, or model minorities who don't have to worry about racism. As a result, too many people dismiss claims of racism and discrimination against Asian Americans and ignore that anti-Asian racism is a part of the systemic racism that has plagued our country since its founding.

History matters. We forget it at our own peril. Georgia state representative Bee Nguyen has said that the history of anti-Asian violence in America has been erased and "not told . . . very intentionally to make us keep our heads down, to pit communities of color against each other, to make us adhere to this model minority myth."

Throughout 2021 and into 2022, Asian Americans gathered to march and bring awareness to the rise in violence against them. They carried signs that said "Stop Anti-Asian Hate!," "I am not a virus," and "I am an American." As has happened numerous times throughout history, Asian Americans were joined by activists of all races, who stood together to call for peace and an end to hatred.

Rally for Asian American women, April 2021.

On May 25, 2020, an African American man named George Floyd was callously murdered by a white police officer in Minneapolis, Minnesota. Just like the police beating of Rodney King in Los Angeles in 1991, the horrific act was caught on video. It was one more racist killing of an African American person by the police force, among far too many. In the summer of 2020, up to 26 million Americans poured into the streets and gathered in front of capitol buildings to call for an end to police violence and justice for African Americans.

Protesters in front of the White House call for change in the wake of the murder of George Floyd, 2020.

Asian Americans joined them, and their protest signs—"Asians 4 Black Lives," "Southeast Asians Believe Black Lives Matter," among others—called specific attention to the importance of interracial support. One of the police officers who stood by without intervening as his colleague took George Floyd's life was an Asian American man. All over the US, Asian Americans took up the call to confront anti-Blackness in the Asian American community. Groups created toolkits called "Fighting Anti-Blackness," they held seminars on how to be good allies, and they organized phone banks to demand that elected leaders take action.

Just as had been the case so many times in the past, it was young people who were the beating heart of these movements for social justice. Asian American teens who were not even old enough to vote were organizing themselves into groups to march, protest, write, and act. These young activists recognized that as the youngest generation of Asian Americans, they had both a responsibility and an opportunity to shape the future of Asian America.

For many of these young people, creating a better future meant confronting the past.

MADE IN ASIAN AMERICA

There is a saying: "History repeats itself."

But that doesn't give human beings enough credit.

In 2021, twelve-year-old Bryan Zhao was feeling pretty nervous. He was sitting in the New Jersey State House, waiting to give his testimony in front of the Senate Education Committee on a bill to require that Asian American history be taught in New Jersey schools. He was the only young person testifying in front of the committee that day.

It's not easy to be the only kid talking to a giant room full of adults.

He took a deep breath, began reading his statement, and took his place in history.

We make history from the courage we show and the truth we speak in the present moment.

In 1983, forty years after the US Supreme Court had ruled

that the incarceration of Japanese Americans was a "military necessity," Fred Korematsu returned to a federal courtroom. He was there to ask the court to overturn his conviction, not just for him personally but for the sake of all Americans. He said, "As long as my record stands in federal court, any American citizen can be held in prison or concentration camps without a trial or a hearing." The judge vacated Korematsu's criminal conviction on the grounds that the Supreme Court had made its decision based on false information.

In the decades since, Fred Korematsu has been celebrated as one of our country's most important civil rights leaders. In 1998, he received the Presidential Medal of Freedom from President Bill Clinton. But he was not done. He spoke up for the liberties of all Americans, including Yaser Hamdi, a Muslim American who, after the 9/11 attacks, was held for years by the US government without trial or access to a lawyer.

We make history when we persevere in the face of difficulty.

When Kala Bagai's husband, Vaishno, took his own life in 1928 after his US citizenship was revoked, Kala was rocked by grief and loss. But eventually, she found the strength to pull herself together. Using the instructions and life insurance policies left behind by Vaishno, she was able to send all three of her children to college. She remarried. In 1946, when the Luce-Celler Act was passed, she was finally able to become a US citizen.

Kala's personal mantra was, "If you are good, the whole world will love you." Kala was warm and supportive to all in her community.

Her home came to be known as a "little India," where South Asians could find each other and make connections with other Americans. As one of the first South Asian women in the United States, she shone a light for the generations who came after her.

In 2020, organizers in Berkeley, California—where the Bagais' racist neighbors had barred them from moving into their home—pushed the city to honor the memory of Kala Bagai. That September, the city council voted unanimously to rename a section of Shattuck Avenue as Kala Bagai Way. Today, banners with Kala's image hang over the downtown street. "Kala Bagai was driven out of Berkeley for her race," said one councilmember on the day the city street was officially renamed. "But today, we are welcoming her back home."

Kala Bagai Way in Berkeley, California.

We make history when we recognize that what we do right now, today, is going to become part of tomorrow's history.

On the day that Bryan Zhao gave his testimony to the New Jersey lawmakers, he was the only young person speaking to the education committee. But actually, his voice was probably the most important one heard that day.

After all, this was a matter of youth education. Who could be more important to hear from than young people themselves? In other public hearings and meetings, Russell Fan, Christina Huang, and Rio Baliga also gave emotional video testimony about why it was so vital that Asian American students learn their own history. They shared their own feelings of being ignored, othered, or unseen.

Dr. Kani Ilangovan knew this feeling well. She had formed an organization to push for this change to New Jersey's history curriculum in response to the rising incidents of hate and violence against Asian Americans. She had partnered with Bryan, Rio, Christina, Kyler, Russell, and other young people to finally get this bill in front of the education committee.

Bryan Zhao presents his eighth-grade curriculum fair project in Princeton, New Jersey, 2023.

Even though Bryan Zhao had been nervous to speak to the committee, once the words started to flow, he felt more confident. It made it easier that he was speaking about something he believed with his whole heart: Asian Americans were a part of America, and everyone deserved to learn about it.

Being a kid in a world where adults move the levers can feel overwhelming. High school junior Ngan Le, who founded the organization Asian Youth Act, has said, "time and time again youth are often ignored . . . they're pushed aside and told 'you don't know enough, you don't have solutions, you can't do that much.'" But their age did not stop Ngan or Bryan or any of the young activists from speaking up. And on January 18, 2022, New Jersey's governor, Phil Murphy, signed the bill incorporating AAPI history into the curriculum, making it a state law.

Now all the students in their state would have the chance to learn about Larry Itliong and Patsy Mink, about Dalip Singh Saund and Mary Tape, about Grace Lee Boggs and Vincent Chin. Earlier that year, the state of Illinois passed a similar bill. The young activists hoped that other states would also get on board.

As difficult and painful as the recent rise in anti-Asian violence had been for Asian Americans, it also felt like an opportunity for real change and reckoning. Cynthia Choi, who cofounded the organization Stop AAPI Hate, has said, "This is a moment for us to really tell that history, to share that not only have Asians and other immigrants and other people of color been blamed and scapegoated, but that there's also a history of our community mobilizing and demanding change and action."

Cynthia, Bryan, Ngan, and other young activists are a product of the struggles, the sacrifices, and the achievements of all the Asian Americans who came before them. This new generation is ready to chart a path forward, to continue the struggle against racism, not just for themselves, but for all Americans.

They are making history—one that is worth repeating.

AUTHOR'S NOTE: ERIKA LEE

I need to make a confession: I never liked history when I was a kid.

I bet you're thinking: Aren't you a historian? Don't you write history books and teach history classes?

It's true. I did not like history when I was growing up. I thought that history was only a timeline of wars and presidents that you had to memorize for a test. It was boring. And it wasn't just about how we learned history; it was what we learned, too: battles that had happened a long time ago and guys in powdered wigs.

In elementary school, we learned about the pilgrims who had come over on the *Mayflower*. We were all in awe of one of my friends whose family history dated back to that time. One of his ancestors had actually sailed over on the *Mayflower* and was a famous leader who was in our history books. My friend got to play his famous ancestor in the school pageant. I got to play his wife.

While I stood in the hot sun in the Puritan-style bonnet that my mother had sewn for me, I remember thinking why my own ancestors—or anybody who looked like me or my Asian American and African American friends—weren't in the history books. And what was our history anyway? Sometimes I would hear the grown-ups talking about how my grandfather came to the United

States when he was sixteen years old and could not speak a word of English. Or how my mother and her sisters competed to see who could make the most egg rolls each afternoon after school for our family restaurant (my aunt May always won). But those were just family *stories*. They weren't *real* history, right?

In high school, I finally had a teacher who made learning about history interesting. Mr. Davis taught us that history wasn't just about the past; it was about the present as well. We studied current events and we analyzed historical documents. We learned about important leaders but also everyday people like women and workers. And even though the class was about European history, I began to realize that history did not have to be boring. And that real people made real history.

But I still could not see how my own family histories fit into the *American* history that I was learning in school. It was like we did not exist as real historical actors, as real history makers. And unlike Plymouth Rock, there were no monuments marking Asian American history as far as I knew. We were invisible in the textbooks and invisible in America.

In college, I was able to take classes on Native American, African American, Latine, and Asian American history for the first time. I learned about the Chinese Exclusion Act of 1882 and Angel Island. I read books by Anne Moody and Louise Erdrich. I met Asian American historians Sucheng Chan and Ronald Takaki, who told me that there were so many more Asian American histories to tell.

Yes, I thought, someone needs to tell these stories! Why aren't there more books, teachers, films, and monuments? Why do we have to wait until we're grown-up to learn our histories? Why can't we learn them in every grade? The more questions I asked, the angrier I got.

And then it struck me: maybe *I* could tell our histories. They would include the stories of my own grandparents' journey to America. And those of other immigrants and refugees, workers, civil rights activists, and changemakers.

So I stayed in school. I read a lot. I learned a lot of American history, world history, and Asian history. And I started to research and write Asian American history. On the weekends, I gave tours of the Angel Island Immigration Station and helped it become a National Historic Landmark. I wrote books about Chinese immigration and about the experiences of immigrants on Angel Island.

When I began teaching students of my own, I realized that there were so many histories yet to be told. My students talked about how they and their parents had escaped persecution in Vietnam, Laos, and Cambodia and were struggling to find their places in America. Their stories were the latest chapters in our diverse history, but they were not yet in our books. I didn't want them to feel lost and invisible in history like I had.

So, in 2015, I wrote *The Making of Asian America: A History* and dedicated it to my students. I wanted them to see their histories represented in the larger story of Asian America and of America. Since its publication, I have had countless conversations with readers telling me that it was the first time that they had ever read anything about their own families and communities. They say that it has helped them understand their parents' (and their own) journeys to the US and their lives in America. It is used in high school and college classrooms. It served as the guide for the Peabody-award-winning film series *Asian Americans*. I thought that my job was done.

Then, during the COVID-19 pandemic, lawmakers and others started to use racist and xenophobic language about the virus. They called the coronavirus the "kung flu" and told Americans to blame China for it. Asian Americans started getting attacked, verbally harassed, and even killed. On March 16, 2021, an armed gunman entered three Asian-owned businesses in the greater Atlanta area and killed eight people. Six were Asian women.

Asian Americans started organizing. They protested against anti-Asian violence and racism. They called on their lawmakers for change. And it wasn't just grown-ups. It was young people as well. In fact, many were leading efforts in their communities to demand Asian American history in their classes. They saw the need for a history education that included all of us, not just some of us. And that the invisibility and erasure of Asian Americans in our history led to ignorance, hate, and violence for Asian American communities today.

More and more people were reading *The Making of Asian America*, and they were asking me if I could write a book for young people. We needed something that could help young people understand the world that they live in today and give them the tools to be active members in their communities during these trying times.

I agreed. But I also knew that I could not do it alone. Then I met editor Jennifer Ung and author Christina Soontornvat. I had just finished reading Christina's *All Thirteen: The Incredible Cave Rescue of the Thai Boys' Soccer Team* and was beginning to read *A Wish in the Dark*. She is an incredible storyteller and advocate, and after just one conversation, I knew that we shared a vision for this book.

We've added more stories and told Asian American history through the experiences of young people, including some of the activists who are inspiring change today. *Made in Asian America: A History for Young People* is the book I wish that I had had when I was growing up.

It is a book about history, about things that happened in the past. But it is also a book about the here and now, and how the world we live in has been shaped by the actions and choices of previous generations. Above all, this book is about people. People doing amazing things under sometimes unimaginable conditions. Taking chances. Making choices to leave, to stay, to fight back, and to imagine different futures.

Their stories are important to share because what they did helps us understand the making of Asian America. And how a new generation—made in Asian America—is drawing inspiration from those who came before them to create a better future for all of us.

AUTHOR'S NOTE: CHRISTINA SOONTORNVAT

I have always loved stories.

I became an author because I loved reading stories and telling stories of my own. As a kid, I always enjoyed learning history because it meant that I got to hear the stories of real people.

But in all my years of K–12 history classes, the only time we focused on stories of Asian Americans was when we discussed the Japanese bombing of Pearl Harbor during World War II. I never read a single book written by an Asian American author in school. At the time, I didn't question any of it. I simply took it for granted that stories of Asians and Asian Americans were missing from both my history and my literature classes. It seemed like this was just the way things were.

Fast-forward a couple of decades, to 2019. By that time, I had found many Asian American authors to read and be inspired by. And some of those authors had started an online book club that I joined. One month, the book club chose to read a history book: *The Making of Asian America* by Dr. Erika Lee. As I read, I flipped the pages faster and faster. I took notes and highlighted passages. It felt like I was trying to drink water from a fire hose. There was *so* much I didn't know. *So* much I had never been taught in school about my own history.

For example, I had never questioned why my father and almost all our Thai American friends and family in the US had immigrated at around the same time in the late 1960s. I had assumed that my dad was a trendsetter! But *The Making of Asian America* taught me this was actually because, after a century of shutting out Asian immigrants, the US passed the 1965 Immigration and Nationality Act, which finally lifted restrictions that changed the lives of so many Asian Americans and literally made my existence possible.

When I finished the book, I felt so many emotions. I was embarrassed that I had made it to forty years old without knowing this information. I felt angry and frustrated that no one had ever taught it to me. I was sad and hurt by all the cruel things humans have done to one another during our country's history. For the first time, I was learning the many ways people of Asian descent have been systematically excluded and discriminated against. It helped me connect the dots to the racism I had personally experienced throughout my life.

Reading Erika's book also gave me a renewed sense of pride in being American. Her pages were filled with inspiring stories, stories of solidarity and allyship, and stories of ordinary people who were true heroes. A big takeaway from the book was that Asian Americans have shaped our nation for the better and have held it to the ideals it was founded on.

I saw how my own personal story was related to the stories of so many people who had come before. Throughout school, I had often felt like I was watching from the margins in history class, but this book showed me how we all fit together. The story of America was so much bigger than what I had been taught.

And so you can guess my reaction when out of the blue, in 2021, I got an email from editor Jennifer Ung, asking if I would like to work with Erika on adapting her original book for young readers. (If you are imagining me screaming and jumping up and down with glee and with tears in my eyes, then you have the right picture.) This felt like it would be one of the most meaningful projects of my career.

While we were making this book, Erika, Jennifer, and I had a lot of conversations. We talked about what we thought all young readers should know about Asian American history, but more than that, we talked about how we wanted young readers to *feel*. We wanted light bulbs to go off. We wanted you to know the truth about our nation's history, and we knew that it would probably make you feel angry, frustrated, and sad at times because we have all felt that same way, too.

We also wanted you to feel inspired by the heroes in these pages. And we want you to feel hopeful for the future because one day very soon, *you* will be the one making history. Ultimately, we hope that every reader who picks up this book feels connected to these stories. These stories are the stories of our nation. And they belong to all of us.

ACKNOWLEDGMENTS

No book is a solo endeavor (especially a collaboration like this one!), and we are so grateful to have had such an incredible team who believed in the project working with us during every stage of the process.

Sarah Park Dahlen, thank you for the early encouragement to create this book, and for all your continued support along the way. Many thanks to Kristen Lee's students at Fletcher Middle School and Ms. Beck's fifth graders at Brentwood Elementary School, who gave us such thoughtful insights during our prewriting focus groups. Tremendous thanks to Soorya "Rio" Baliga, Russell Fan, Ngan Le, Serena Lee, Bryan Zhao, and Kyler Zhou for sharing their inspiring stories of activism and resilience with us.

Thank you so much to Eleana Kim, Helen Zia, Kao Kalia Yang, Deann Borshay, Kim Park Nelson, Yifeng Hu, Wendy Chou Le, and Simran Jeet Singh for reviewing selected chapters and providing your photos and expertise. Ashley Duffey, thank you for your valuable help during the photo research process.

We are tremendously grateful for all the support from the HarperCollins team. Courtney Stevenson, you deserve a medal for all your work on our photo collection. Thank you to artist Gica

Tam, designer Kathy Lam, and art director David Curtis for our gorgeous cover illustration and design. Many thanks to our heroic production editor, Caitlin Lonning, and copyeditor, Jessica White. Thank you to Sabrina Abballe, Robby Imfeld, Anna Ravenelle, Patty Rosati, Kerry Moynagh, Rosemary Brosnan, and Suzanne Murphy for championing this book and helping it find its way to readers. Finally, an enormous thank-you to our wonderful editor, Jennifer Ung, who has guided this book with a steady hand and a passionate heart throughout its journey. Her vision, leadership, and commitment to this project have meant the world to us.

From Erika: Thank you to my literary agent, Sandy Dijkstra, as well as Elise Capron, Thao Le, and the rest of the team at the Dijkstra Literary Agency for helping to make this incredible book adaptation possible and for all your support along the way. My deepest thanks to my family—Laurel, Kristen, Dad, Molly, Mark, Ben, and Billy—for your love and support. It means so much to me and keeps me going every day. Lastly, I am so incredibly grateful to have worked with the amazing Christina Soontornvat on this book and for her bringing her powerful voice and eloquence to our histories.

From Christina: Thank you to my literary agent, Stephanie Fretwell-Hill, for helping make this dream project a reality. So much gratitude to dear friends Ellen Oh, Minh Lê, and Hena Khan for always being there. All my love to my family: Mom, Bob, Dad, Liz, Tom, Elowyn, and Aven for the unwavering support. Finally, I am forever grateful to Erika Lee—for writing such an impactful book, and for trusting me to work with her on this one.

SOURCE NOTES

INTRODUCTION

"There was essentially . . . yourself in a way.": Erika Lee interview with Soorya "Rio" Baliga, May 13, 2022.

"This pandemic wouldn't . . . where you belong!": Russell Jeung, Tara Popovic, Richard Lim, Nelson Lin, "Anti-Chinese Rhetoric Employed by Perpetrators of Anti-Asian Hate," Stop AAPI Hate, October 11, 2020. stopaapihate.org/2020/10/11 /anti-chinese-rhetoric-employed-by-perpetrators-of-anti-asian -hate.

"You brought the virus on purpose!": Russell Jeung, Tara Popovic, Richard Lim, Nelson Lin, "Anti-Chinese Rhetoric Employed by Perpetrators of Anti-Asian Hate," Stop AAPI Hate, October 11, 2020. stopaapihate.org/2020/10/11/anti-chinese-rhetoric -employed-by-perpetrators-of-anti-asian-hate.

"Kill all Asians.": Hanna Park, "He Shot at 'Everyone He Saw': Atlanta Spa Workers Recount Horrors of Shooting," NBC News, April 2, 2021. www.nbcnews.com/news/asian-america /he-shot-everyone-he-saw-atlanta-spa-workers-recount -horrors-n1262928.

CHAPTER 2: FOLLOWING THE
ROUTES OF EMPIRE: ASIANS IN "NEW SPAIN"

"Castles in the sea": William Lytle Schurz, *The Manila Galleon* (New York: E. P. Dutton & Co., Inc., 1959), 195–97.

"A racist idea is any idea . . . a racial group.": Jason Reynolds and Ibram X. Kendi, *Stamped: Racism, Antiracism, and You* (New York: Little, Brown Books for Young Readers, 2020).

CHAPTER 3: BROKEN PROMISES:
AFONG MOY AND THE STRUGGLES OF ASIAN LABORERS

"Curiosities" . . . "unprecedented novelty": Linda Kimiko August, "Remembering Afong Moy," The Library Company of Philadelphia, librarycompany.org/2021/02/01/remembering-afong-moy.

"Leased convicts": Neal Conan, "The Untold History of Post-Civil War 'Neoslavery,'" NPR, March 25, 2008. www.npr.org/transcripts/89051115.

"Debt slavery": "Slavery v. Peonage," PBS. www.pbs.org/tpt/slavery-by-another-name/themes/peonage.

"More akin to the monkey than to man.": Hugh Tinker, *A New System of Slavery* (London: Oxford University Press, 1974), 19, 63.

"I had to labor night and day . . . imprisoned for resting a few moments.": China Cuba Commission, *The Cuba Commission Report* (Baltimore: Johns Hopkins University Press, 1993), 56.

CHAPTER 4: IN SEARCH OF GOLD MOUNTAIN:
MAMIE TAPE AND THE FIRST CHINESE IN AMERICA

"Americans are very rich people . . . and to spare in America.":

Xiao-huang Yin, *Chinese American Literature Since the 1850s* (Urbana: University of Illinois Press, 2000), 14.

"Without them it would . . . this great National highway.": Edwin Legrand Sabin, *Building the Pacific Railway: The Construction-Story of America's First Iron Thoroughfare Between the Missouri River and California, from the Inception of the Great Idea to the Day, May 10, 1869, When the Union Pacific and the Central Pacific Joined Tracks at Promontory Point, Utah, to Form the Nation's Transcontinental* (Philadelphia: J. B. Lippincott, 1919), 111.

"It is only in Chinatown . . . his hardships and adventures.": Ching Chao Wu, "Chinatowns: A Study of Symbiosis and Assimilation" (PhD diss., University of Chicago, 1928), 158.

"I see that you are going to . . . keep her out.": Heather Thomas, "Before *Brown v. Board of Education*, There Was *Tape v. Hurley*," *Headlines and Heroes* (blog), Library of Congress Blogs (May 5, 2021), blogs.loc.gov/headlinesandheroes/2021/05/before-brown-v-education-there-was-tape-v-hurley.

"Filthy or vicious habits . . . infectious diseases.": Mae M. Ngai, *The Lucky Ones: One Family and the Extraordinary Invention of Chinese America* (Boston: Houghton Mifflin Harcourt, 2010), 43–57.

CHAPTER 5: ONE THOUSAND QUESTIONS: TYRUS WONG, ANGEL ISLAND, AND CHINESE EXCLUSION

"What direction . . . all your family members?": "Imagine an Immigration Interview," Smithsonian National Museum of

American History. amhistory.si.edu/ourstory/pdf/immigration
/immigration_interview.pdf.

"Machine-like" . . . "muscles of iron.": Andrew Gyory, *Closing the Gate: Race, Politics, and the Chinese Exclusion Act* (Chapel Hill NC: The University of North Carolina Press, 1998), 223–38.

"a plague spot" . . . "laboratory of infection": Nayan Shah, *Contagious Divides: Epidemics and Race in San Francisco's Chinatown* (Berkeley: University of California Press, 2001), 1–2.

"Degraded and inferior race," "rats," "beasts," "swine": Gyory, *Closing the Gate*, 223–38.

"It was just like jail.": Rosalind Chang, "A Profile of Tyrus Wong," Immigrant Voices, Angel Island Immigration Station Foundation, www.immigrant-voices.aiisf.org/stories-by-author/587-wong-tyrus-3.

"There are tens of thousands of poems . . . that this chapter once existed.": Him Mark Lai, Genny Lim, and Judy Yung, eds., *Island: Poetry and History of Chinese Immigrants on Angel Island, 1910–1940*, 2nd ed. (Seattle: University of Washington Press, 2014), 66.

WHO GETS TO BE AN AMERICAN?

"Utterly unfit": Erika Lee, "*Wong Kim Ark v. United States*: Immigration, Race, and Citizenship," in *Race Law Stories*, Devon Carbado and Rachel Moran, eds. (New York: Foundation Press, 2008), 91, 95.

CHAPTER 6: UNWAVERING: MARY PAIK LEE

"We have no country to return to. We are a conquered people.":
Ronald T. Takaki, *Strangers from a Different Shore: A History of Asian Americans* (Boston: Little, Brown, 1998), 282.

"Now that I look back . . . how much work was ahead.": Takaki, *Strangers from a Different Shore*, 137.

"Why did we come to a place where we were not wanted?" "Anything new and strange . . . violence result.": Mary Paik Lee, *Quiet Odyssey: A Pioneer Korean Woman in America*, ed. Sucheng Chan (Seattle: University of Washington Press, 2019), 13.

"Korea was a wild, savage country.": Paik Lee, *Quiet Odyssey*, 105,

"Speak up . . . for what is right.": Paik Lee, *Quiet Odyssey*, 44.

CHAPTER 7: STEADFAST SURVIVORS: THE BAGAI FAMILY

"First Hindu woman": Kritika Agarwal, "Kala Bagai," "Our Stories: An Introduction to South Asian America," South Asian American Digital Archive (2021), 65–70.

"I don't want to stay in this slave country . . . America where there is no slavery.": Rani Bagai, "Bridges Burnt Behind: The Story of Vaishno Das Bagai and Kala Bagai," Immigrant Voices, Angel Island Immigration Station Foundation, www.immigrant-voices .aiisf.org/stories-by-author/876-bridges-burnt-behind-the-story -of-vaishno-das-bagai (accessed July 25, 2023).

"Roughest most unskilled work.": H. A. Millis, "East Indian Immigration to British Columbia and the Pacific Coast States," *American Economic Review* 1, no. 1 (March 1911): 74.

"I don't want to live in . . . I don't want it.": Bagai, "Bridges Burnt Behind."

"Universally regarded as the least desirable . . . to the United States.": US Senate, *Reports of the Immigration Commission: Immigrants in Industries, Part 25: Japanese and Other Immigrant Races in the Pacific Coast and Rocky Mountain States, vol. 1: Japanese and East Indians* (Washington, DC: US Government Printing Office, 1911), 349.

"Drive out the Hindus.": *Bellingham Herald*, September 5, 1907.

"Hindu Invasion" . . . "Tide of Turbans": "Turn Back the Hindu Invasion," *San Francisco Call*, February 1, 1910; Herman Scheffauer, "The Tide of Turbans," *The Forum*, vol. 43 (June 1910), 616–618.

"Now what am I? . . . bridges burnt behind.": Vaishno Das Bagai, "Here's Letter to the World from Suicide," *San Francisco Examiner*, March 17, 1928.

CHAPTER 8: AN ALL-AMERICAN GIRL: MONICA ITOI SONE

"Aliens ineligible for citizenship": Roger Daniels, *The Politics of Prejudice: The Anti-Japanese Movement in California and the Struggle for Japanese Exclusion* (Berkeley: University of California Press, 1962), 63.

"White in color": Ian F. Haney López, *White by Law: The Legal Construction of Race* (New York: New York University Press, 1996), 56–61.

"In name, I am not an American . . . a true American.": Haney López, *White by Law*, 56–61.

"Sorry, we don't want any Japs around here." . . . "We're not 'Japs.' We're American citizens.": Monica Sone, *Nisei Daughter* (Seattle: University of Washington Press, 2014), 119.

CHAPTER 9: ALREADY AMERICAN: FRANCISCO CARIÑO

"Little brown brothers": Yen Le Espiritu, *Home Bound: Filipino American Lives across Cultures, Communities, and Countries* (Berkeley: University of California Press, 2003), 46–62.

"A land of the brave and the free, land of opportunity" . . . "a land of Paradise.": Francisco Cariño, "My Life History," August 1924, Survey of Race Relations, Major Document No. 85, Hoover Institution Archives, Stanford University.

"Are you a Jap?" . . . "I'm sorry—you are dark." . . . "Positively No Filipinos Allowed" . . . "No Filipinos or Dogs.": Cariño, "My Life History."

"When asparagus is over here . . . I just wanted to work.": Interview with Eliseo Felipe by Judy Yung, April 23, 2009, cited in Lee and Yung, *Angel Island: Immigrant Gateway to America* (New York: Oxford University Press, 2010), 278–79.

"People have no biological differences . . . in one golden cord of love.": Cariño, "My Life History."

CHAPTER 10: MILITARY NECESSITY: THE INCARCERATION OF JAPANESE AMERICANS

"Pearl Harbor has been bombed! . . . The Japanese are bombing Pearl Harbor!" "Because obviously the pilot in that plane looked like me.": "Sen. Daniel Inouye on Pearl Harbor, After

70 Years," *Tell Me More*, NPR News, December 7, 2011, www.npr.org/2011/12/07/143271323/sen-daniel-inouye-on -pearl-harbor-after-70-years.

"Eager to show their loyalty.": John Franklin Carter, "Memorandum on C. B. Munson's Report 'Japanese on the West Coast,'" November 7, 1941, Commission on Wartime Relocation and Internment of Civilians, Densho ID: denshopd-i67-00011, Densho Digital Repository (accessed March 19, 2013).

"The most effective fifth column work of the entire war.": Greg Robinson, *A Tragedy of Democracy: Japanese Confinement in North America* (New York: Columbia University Press, 2009), 62.

"The Japanese race is an enemy race." . . . "The very fact no sabotage . . . action *will* be taken." Commission on Wartime Relocation and Internment of Civilians, *Personal Justice Denied* (Washington, DC: Civil Liberties Public Education Fund; Seattle: University of Washington Press, 1997), 66, 82.

"Why should that bother me? . . . I no longer felt I'm an equal American.": Akiko Kurose Interview I, Segment 13, July 17, 1997, Densho Visual History Collection, Densho Digital Archive, ddr.densho.org/media/ddr-densho-1000/ddr-densho -1000-41-transcript-3d1725e567.htm (accessed May 22, 2013).

"Herd 'em up, pack 'em off. . . then let the million innocents suffer.": Henry McLemore, "This Is War! Stop Worrying About Hurting Jap Feelings," *Seattle Times*, January 30, 1942.

CHAPTER 11: "GOOD" ASIANS, "BAD" ASIANS

"All at once we discovered . . . how good they were.": *Congressional*

Record, 78th Cong., 1st Sess., 1943, vol. 89, part 6, 8594.

"All of a sudden . . . an American Dream.": Kevin Scott Wong, *Americans First: Chinese Americans and the Second World War* (Cambridge: Harvard University Press, 2005), 204.

"China is our ally. . . . Today, we fight at her side.": "An Act to Repeal the Chinese Exclusion Acts, to Establish Quotas, and for Other Purposes," Act of Dec. 17, 1943 (57 Stat. 600; 8 U.S.C. 212a).

"Day that will live in infamy.": "FDR's 'Day of Infamy' Speech: Crafting a Call to Arms," Our Heritage in Documents, *Prologue* 33, no. 4 (Winter 2001), US National Archives, www.archives.gov/publications/prologue/2001/winter/crafting-day-of-infamy-speech.html.

"We Filipinos are the same . . . their recognition of us.": Manuel Buaken, *I Have Lived with the American People* (Caldwell, ID: Caxton, 1948), 322–23.

"There's one of them . . . Japs now." . . . "Shame on you . . . " " . . . beat up a one-year-old baby?": Paik Lee, *Quiet Odyssey*, 95.

"Many [Koreans] were beaten during the day. . . . It was a bad time for all of us.": Paik Lee, *Quiet Odyssey*, 95–96.

CHAPTER 12: LOYALTY

"Would you be willing to swear . . . power or organization?": Frank Miyamoto Interview III, Segment 21, April 29, 1998, Densho Visual History Collection, Densho Digital Archive, ddr.densho.org/interviews/ddr-densho-1000-52-21 (accessed May 11, 2013).

"Are you willing to serve . . . wherever ordered?": Cherstin Lyon.

"Questions 27 and 28," Densho Encyclopedia, encyclopedia
.densho.org/Questions%2027%20and%2028 (accessed July
27, 2023).

"Human secret weapon for the US Armed Forces.": "Military
Intelligence Service," Go for Broke National Education Center,
goforbroke.org/military-intelligence-service.

"One instant he was standing waist-high . . . a fist that suddenly
didn't belong to me anymore.": "Medal of Honor Recipient Daniel Inouye Led a Life of Service to His Country,"
The National World War II Museum, July 19, 2020, www
.nationalww2museum.org/war/articles/medal-of-honor
-recipient-daniel-inouye.

"The fighting was really fierce. . . . it burst like geysers.": Fred
Matsumura, Segment 20, July 2, 1998, Densho Visual History
Collection, Densho Digital Archive, ddr.densho.org/interviews
/ddr-densho-1000-46-20 (accessed December 16, 2014).

"I didn't feel guilty. . . . I had as many rights as anyone else.":
Richard Goldstein, "Fred Korematsu, 86, dies; Lost Key Suit
on Internment," *New York Times*, April 1, 2005.

"When the war came . . . the Issei who've struggled so much for
us.": Sone, *Nisei Daughter*, 236.

CHAPTER 13: IMPOSSIBLE DREAMS: DEANN BORSHAY

"When I was younger . . . be with my Korean family." "I had been
given . . . didn't belong to me.": Deann Borshay (dir.), *First
Person Plural*, 2000.

"You hope that retracing . . . leads to more questions.": Lisa

Wool-Rim Sjöblom, *Palimpsest: Documents from a Korean Adoption* (Montreal: Drawn and Quarterly, 2019), 96.

"My childhood fantasy . . . my Korean family.": Borshay, *First Person Plural*.

CHAPTER 14: SOLIDARITY: THE ONGOING FIGHT FOR CIVIL RIGHTS

"I began to take a serious interest . . . to fight for my civil rights, too.": Yuri Kochiyama, *Passing It On: A Memoir* (Los Angeles: UCLA Asian American Studies Center Press, 2004), 45.

"Black people must recognize . . . brothers and sisters.": "Bayard Rustin and Asian America," See Us Unite Video Project, www.youtube.com/watch?v=YGYRdv3UXgM.

"When I saw what a movement could do . . . with my life.": Bill Moyers, "Grace Lee Boggs," *Bill Moyers Journal*, PBS, June 15, 2007, www.pbs.org/moyers/journal/06152007/profile2.html (accessed October 18, 2011).

"The first camp I lived in . . . so full that it was impossible to use.": Kent Wong, "United Farm Workers (UFW) Movement: Philip Vera Cruz, Unsung Hero," UCLA Asian American Studies Center, www.aasc.ucla.edu/resources/untoldstories/UCRS_Philip_Vera_Cruz_r2.pdf.

"I said, 'Please, Malcolm! Please, Malcolm! Stay alive!'": "Civil Rights Activist Yuri Kochiyama on Her Internment in a WWII Japanese American Detention Camp & Malcolm X's Assassination," Democracy Now!, February 20, 2008, www.democracynow.org/2008/2/20/civil_rights_activist_yuri_kochiyama_remembers.

"Well, in your country, you are lynching African Americans.": Jelani Cobb, "The Enduring Russian Propaganda Interests in Targeting African-Americans," *New Yorker*, December 21, 2018, www .newyorker.com/news/daily-comment/the-enduring-russian -propaganda-interests-in-targeting-african-americans.

CHAPTER 15: AMERICA'S GATES REOPEN: THE 1965 IMMIGRATION AND NATIONALITY ACT

"This bill we sign . . . the shape of our daily lives.": Tom Gjelten, "In 1965, a Conservative Tried to Keep America White. His Plan Backfired," WBUR Boston, October 3, 2015, www.wbur.org /npr/445339838/the-unintended-consequences-of-the-1965 -immigration-act.

"Hordes" . . . "dumping ground": David M. Reimers, *Still the Golden Door: The Third World Comes to America* (New York: Columbia University Press, 1985), 81.

CHAPTER 16: THE MYTHICAL MODEL MINORITY

"Asian Americans . . . most highly regarded schools.": Dennis William et al., "A Formula for Success," *Newsweek*, April 23, 1984.

"America's Super Minority" . . . "smarter and better educated and make more money than everyone else" "Asian Americans . . . smarter than the rest of us.": Anthony Ramirez, "America's Super Minority," *Fortune*, November 24, 1986.

CHAPTER 17: FIRSTS AND FLYING FISTS

"There's no way . . . fight Robin and lose.": James Ellis, "The Kato

Show: Bruce Lee as the Green Hornet's Sidekick," *Newsweek*, November 20, 2015, www.newsweek.com/bruce-lee-king-fu -martial-arts-390811.

"The lovely Oriental doll of a delegate from Hawai'i.": Judy Tzu-Chun Wu and Gwendolyn Mink, *Fierce and Fearless: Patsy Takemoto Mink, First Woman of Color in Congress* (New York: New York University Press, 2022), 77.

"I hoped and prayed . . . germs of a discriminating nature.": Tzu-Chun Wu and Mink, *Fierce and Fearless*, 36.

"Look at me . . . living proof of America's democracy.": "Made in America," *Time*, January 9, 1956; "Jackie and the Judge," *Time*, February 27, 1956; "Living Proof," *Time*, November 19, 1956.

"Spokesman for Asian Americans across the country.": "Fong, Hiram Leong: Biography," US House of Representatives History, Art, and Archives, history.house.gov/People/Detail /15032451315.

"I had not yet come out . . . for the next several years.": Helen Zia, "Where the Queer Zone Meets the Asian Zone: Marriage Equality and Other Intersections," *Amerasia Journal 32*, no. 1 (January 1, 2006): 3.

"I can finally say I am not ashamed anymore. . . . all that I signed up to do.": Dan Choi, "Dan Choi," *The Atlantic*, November 2010, www.theatlantic.com/magazine/archive/2010/11/dan -choi/308278.

"She has brown eyes . . . five feet, one and a half inches tall." "It is easy enough to vote . . . stand alone for a while if necessary.":

Tzu-Chun Wu and Mink, *Fierce and Fearless*, 84.

"No person in the United States shall . . . activity receiving Federal financial assistance.": Megan Cole, "Title IX's Legacy at 50," UC Irvine School of Humanities, April 14, 2022, www .humanities.uci.edu/news/title-ixs-legacy-50.

CHAPTER 18: SEEKING REFUGE: SOUTHEAST ASIAN AMERICANS

"I was born in Vietnam . . . and breathed war.": Sucheng Chan, *The Vietnamese American 1.5 Generation* (Philadelphia: Temple University Press, 2006), 97.

"Only in unpopulated parts of Cambodia.": Kenton Clymer, "Cambodia and Laos in the Vietnam War," *The Columbia History of the Vietnam War* (New York: Columbia University Press, 2010): 373; Ben Kiernan, "The American Bombardment of Kampuchea, 1969–1973," *Vietnam Generation* 1, no. 1 (Winter 1989): 6, 8.

"I felt myself falling apart . . . everything I had loved.": Chan, *The Vietnamese American 1.5 Generation*, 104–12.

"As soon as the airplane lands . . . step on each other to get in the plane." "Everyone cried . . . like thin air.": Chia Youyee Vang, *Hmong America: Reconstructing Community in Diaspora* (Champaign, IL: University of Illinois Press, 2010), 36.

"It's hard to present yourself . . . or dial the phone.": Lillian Faderman and Ghia Xiong, *I Begin My Life All Over* (Boston: Beacon Press, 1999), 164.

"We already have too many Orientals.": Gail Paradise Kelly,

From Vietnam to America: A Chronicle of the Vietnamese Immigration to the United States (Boulder, CO: Westview, 1977), 18.

"Next to waves of hello, we received the middle finger.": Kao Kalia Yang, *The Latehomecomer: A Hmong Family Memoir* (Minneapolis: Coffee House Press, 2008), 133.

"Been loyal Americans before they even set foot on American soil,": Vang, *Hmong America*, 123, 129.

CHAPTER 19: "IT'S BECAUSE OF YOU"– THE MURDER OF VINCENT CHIN

"It's because of . . . that we're out of work!": Helen Zia and the Vincent Chin Institute, "The Vincent Chin Legacy Guide: Asian Americans and Civil Rights," 2022, 12.

"As if he were going for a home run.": Zia and the Vincent Chin Institute, "The Vincent Chin Legacy Guide," 13.

"They weren't the kind of people . . . the punishment fit the criminal.": Paula Yoo, *From a Whisper to a Rallying Cry: The Killing of Vincent Chin and the Trial That Galvanized the Asian American Movement* (New York: Norton Young Readers, 2021), 62.

"Datsun, Toyota, Nissan. Remember Pearl Harbor!": Yoo, *From a Whisper to a Rallying Cry*, 43.

"Why don't you go back to Japan with the cars.": Yoo, *From a Whisper to a Rallying Cry*, 48.

"The little yellow people.": Yoo, *From a Whisper to a Rallying Cry*, 48.

"If I were president . . . I'd fix the Japanese like they have never been fixed.": Yoo, *From a Whisper to a Rallying Cry*, 49.

"It felt dangerous . . . if they were thought to be Japanese.": Yoo, *From a Whisper to a Rallying Cry*, 43.

"The stereotype that Asians in America . . . to go free." "If you talk to . . . That case changed my life.": Yoo, *From a Whisper to a Rallying Cry*, 295.

"My experience as a Hmong refugee was connected to the experience of other Asian Americans.": Renee Tajima-Peña (prod.), *Asian Americans*, PBS, 2020.

CHAPTER 20: LEFT TO BURN: KOREATOWN ON SA I GU

"I had never seen Koreans on TV . . . in front of their burned-down stores.": Grace Lee, *K-Town'92*, ktown92.com.

CHAPTER 21: "LOOKING LIKE THE ENEMY"

"Hey, little terrorist . . . knives in there, are you?": Simran Jeet Singh, *The Light We Give: How Sikh Wisdom Can Transform Your Life* (New York: Riverhead Books, 2022), 2.

"Complete and total shutdown of Muslims.": Jessica Taylor, "Trump Calls for 'Total and Complete Shutdown of Muslims Entering' U.S.," NPR, December 7, 2015, www.npr.org /2015/12/07/458836388/trump-calls-for-total-and-complete -shutdown-of-muslims-entering-u-s.

"Boost public morale.": US War Relocation Authority, "Background for the Relocation Program," 1942, War Relocation Authority Collection, Special Collections and Archives, University Library, California State University, Northridge, Densho Digital

Repository, ddr.densho.org/ddr-csujad-19-34.

"The same bad logic of the 1940s decision . . . one injustice with another.": Karen Korematsu, "How the Supreme Court Replaced One Injustice with Another," *New York Times*, June 27, 2018, www.nytimes.com/2018/06/27/opinion/supreme-court-travel-ban-korematsu-japanese-internment.html.

"I'll always remember my . . . more love there is in the world than hate.": Jeet Singh, *The Light We Give*, 37.

"We needed to grow up . . . warriors of our communities.": Sasha von Oldershausen, "How Growing Up in New York After 9/11 Shaped These Muslim Leaders," *New York Times*, September 11, 2021, www.nytimes.com/2021/09/10/nyregion/sept-11-muslim-new-york.html.

"The trick is to recognize . . . none of us lives beyond the present.": Jeet Singh, *The Light We Give*, 77.

CHAPTER 22: ASIAN AMERICAN RECKONINGS

"China is to blame . . . and things like that.": Kyler Zhou, "The Sinophobia Outbreak." *Hear Our Voices*, December 13, 2020.

CHAPTER 23: MADE IN ASIAN AMERICA

"As long as my record . . . without a trial or a hearing.": Shiho Imai, "*Korematsu v. United States*," Densho Encyclopedia, encyclopedia.densho.org/Korematsu_v._United_States/ (accessed July 25, 2023).

"If you are good, the whole world will love you.": South Asian American Digital Archive, *Our Stories: An Introduction to*

South Asian America (South Asian American Digital Archive, 2022), 65–70.

"Kala Bagai was driven out of Berkeley . . . we are welcoming her back home.": Katia Pokotylo, "Downtown Berkeley Street Renamed after South Asian Immigrant Kala Bagai," *Daily Californian*, February 11, 2021.

"Time and time again youth are often ignored . . . they're pushed aside and told 'you don't know enough, you don't have solutions, you can't do that much.'": Erika Lee interview with Ngan Le, May 16, 2022.

"This is a moment for us . . . demanding change and action.": Jerusalem Demsas and Rachel Ramirez, "The History of Tensions—and Solidarity—Between Black and Asian American Communities, Explained," Vox, March 16, 2021, www.vox.com/22321234/black-asian-american-tensions-solidarity-history.

BIBLIOGRAPHY

"10 Little Known Facts About Life at Minidoka," Densho, August 6, 2019, densho.org/catalyst/10-little-known-facts-of-life-at -minidoka.

"1830–1860: Diplomacy and Westward Expansion," US Department of State Office of the Historian. history.state.gov /milestones/1830-1860/foreword.

"Adoption History," *First Person Plural* Original Website. Firstpersonplural.mufilms.org/historical.php.

Agarwal, Kritika. "Kala Bagai," "Our Stories: An Introduction to South Asian America." South Asian American Digital Archive, 2021. www.saada.org/ourstories/readers/chapter-2.

Agarwal, Kritika. "Living in a Gilded Cage," South Asian American Digital Archive, August 6, 2014. www.saada.org/tides /article/living-in-a-gilded-cage.

Alexander, Kerri Lee. "Anna May Wong," National Women's History Museum. www.womenshistory.org/education-resources /biographies/anna-may-wong.

"Angel Island Profile: Tyrus Wong," Angel Island Immigration Station Foundation and Leapman Productions, YouTube video. www.youtube.com/watch?v=5rz5whByOts.

Astor, Gerald. *Crisis in the Pacific: The Battles for the Philippine Islands by the Men Who Fought Them*. New York: Dell, 2002.

August, Linda Kimiko. "Remembering Afong Moy," The Library Company of Philadelphia. librarycompany.org/2021/02/01/remembering-afong-moy.

"Bilali (Ben Ali) Muhammad's Diary," Discover Africa in the Americas, Howard University. africaaccessreview.org/http-discoverafricaintheworld-org/united-states/discover-africa-in-georgia/bilai-muhammad.

Borshay, Deann (dir.). *First Person Plural*, 2000.

Brown, Patricia Leigh. "Forgotten Hero of Labor Fight; His Son's Lonely Quest," *New York Times*, October 18, 2012. www.nytimes.com/2012/10/19/us/larry-itliong-forgotten-filipino-labor-leader.html.

"Bruce Lee Bio," Bruce Lee Family Company. brucelee.com/bruce-lee.

"Bruce Lee Steals the Show in 'The Green Hornet,'" *Discover History* (blog), American Heritage Center, March 16, 2020. ahcwyo.org/2020/03/16/bruce-lee-steals-the-show-in-the-green-hornet.

Buchanan, Larry, Quoctrung Bui, and Jugal K. Patel. "Black Lives Matter May Be the Largest Movement in U.S. History," *New York Times*, July 3, 2020. www.nytimes.com/interactive/2020/07/03/us/george-floyd-protests-crowd-size.html.

Cariño, Francisco. "My Life History," August 1924, Survey of Race Relations, Major Document No. 85, Hoover Institution Library and Archives, Stanford University.

"Central Europe Campaign," Go for Broke National Education Center. goforbroke.org/central-europe-campaign.

Chang, Rosalind. "A Profile of Tyrus Wong," Immigrant Voices, Angel Island Immigration Station Foundation. www .immigrant-voices.aiisf.org/stories-by-author/587-wong-tyrus-3.

Choi, Dan. "Dan Choi," *The Atlantic*, November 2010. www .theatlantic.com/magazine/archive/2010/11/dan-choi/308278.

Chong, Raymond Douglas. "Chinese Immigration and the Legend-ary Frederick Douglass," AsAmNews, June 17, 2021. asamnews .com/2021/06/17/civil-rights-pioneer-frederick-douglass -opposed-immigration-laws-which-restricted-chinese-and -japanese-from-coming-to-the-u-s.

Chow, Kat. "If We Called Ourselves Yellow," *Code Switch* (blog), NPR, September 27, 2018. www.npr.org/sections /codeswitch/2018/09/27/647989652/if-we-called-ourselves-yellow.

"Civil Rights Activist Yuri Kochiyama on Her Internment in a WWII Japanese American Detention Camp & Malcolm X's Assassination," Democracy Now!, February 20, 2008. www .democracynow.org/2008/2/20/civil_rights_activist_yuri _kochiyama_remembers.

Cobb, Jelani. "The Enduring Russian Propaganda Interests in Targeting African-Americans," *New Yorker*, December 21, 2018. www.newyorker.com/news/daily-comment/the-enduring -russian-propaganda-interests-in-targeting-african-americans.

Cole, Megan. "Title IX's Legacy at 50," UC Irvine School of Humanities, April 14, 2022. www.humanities.uci.edu/news /title-ixs-legacy-50.

Constante, Agnes, and Natasha Roy. "75 Ways Asian Americans and Pacific Islanders Are Speaking Out for Black Lives," NBC News, June 12, 2020. www.nbcnews.com/news /asian-america/75-ways-asian-americans-pacific-islanders-are -speaking-out-black-n1230551.

Davis, Nancy E. *The Chinese Lady: Afong Moy in Early America.* New York: Oxford University Press, 2019.

"Decolonization of Asia and Africa, 1945–1960," US Department of State Office of the Historian, 2001–2009. history.state.gov /milestones/1945-1952/asia-and-africa.

Deliso, Meredith. "At Dozens of Rallies, Protesters Call for End to Anti-Asian Violence," ABC News, March 27, 2021. abcnews .go.com/US/dozens-rallies-protesters-call-end-anti-asian -violence/story?id=76727278.

Ellis, James. "The Kato Show: Bruce Lee as the Green Hornet's Sidekick," *Newsweek*, November 20, 2015. www.newsweek .com/bruce-lee-king-fu-martial-arts-390811.

Fam, Mariam, Deepti Hajela, and Luis Andres Henao. "Two Decades After 9/11, Muslim Americans Still Fighting Bias," AP News, September 7, 2021. apnews.com/article/September-11 -Muslim-Americans-93f97dd9219c25371428f4268a2b33b4.

"Fears and Concerns of Affected, At-Risk Communities," Chapter 6 of Civil Rights Concerns in the Metropolitan Washington, D.C., Area in the Aftermath of the September 11, 2001, Tragedies, US Commission on Civil Rights. www.usccr.gov/files /pubs/sac/dc0603/ch6.htm.

"Fong, Hiram Leong: Biography," US House of Representatives

History, Art, and Archives. history.house.gov/People /Detail/15032451315.

Fox, Margalit. "Tyrus Wong, 'Bambi' Artist Thwarted by Racial Bias, Dies at 106," *New York Times*, December 30, 2016. www.nytimes.com/2016/12/30/movies/tyrus-wong-dies -bambi-disney.html.

Fujino, Diane C. "Yuri Kochiyama," Densho Encyclopedia. encyclopedia.densho.org/Yuri%20Kochiyama.

Gandhi, Lakshmi. "The Asian American Women Who Fought to Make Their Mark in WWII," History Channel, May 3, 2021. www.history.com/news/asian-american-women-wwii -contributions.

Gjelten, Tom. "In 1965, a Conservative Tried to Keep America White. His Plan Backfired," WBUR Boston, October 3, 2015. www.wbur.org/npr/445339838/the-unintended-consequences -of-the-1965-immigration-act.

Godoy, Maria. "Lo Mein Loophole: How U.S. Immigration Law Fueled a Chinese Restaurant Boom," *The Salt* (blog), NPR, February 22, 2016. www.npr.org/sections/thesalt/2016/02/22/467113401 /lo-mein-loophole-how-u-s-immigration-law-fueled-a-chinese -restaurant-boom.

Gururaja, Kamala. "My Name Is Poonam Gulati Salhotra," SAADA First Days Project. firstdays.saada.org/story/poonam -gulati-salhotra.

Hinckley, Story. "Yuri Kochiyama: A Nisei Ahead of Her Time," Christian Science Monitor, May 19, 2016, www.csmonitor.com/USA /Society/2016/0519/Yuri-Kochiyama-a-nisei-ahead-of-her-time.

"History Blueprint: Cold War America Lesson 2: Containing Communism Abroad," UC Davis. chssp.ucdavis.edu/sites/g /files/dgvnsk8426/files/inline-files/Containment%20Abroad%20 %28CWA2%29.pdf.

"Hmong History," Hmong American Center. www .hmongamericancenter.org/hmong-history.

"Imagine an Immigration Interview," Smithsonian National Museum of American History. amhistory.si.edu/ourstory/pdf /immigration/immigration_interview.pdf.

"Interview with Dr. Poonam Gulati Salhotra," Houston Asian American Archive—Oral History Collection, November 28, 2020, YouTube video. youtu.be/dLicbiMhh_0.

Jacobs, Sally. "50 Years Later, the Couple at the Heart of *Loving v. Virginia* Still Stirs Controversy," WGBH Educational Foundation, June 11, 2017. www.wgbh.org/news/2017/06/11 /news/50-years-later-couple-heart-loving-v-virginia-still-stirs -controversy.

Jeffreys, Alan. "Decolonisation in South East and South Asia, 1945–1948," Imperial War Museums. www.iwm.org.uk /history/britain-and-decolonisation-in-south-east-and-south -asia-1945-1948.

Kendi, Ibram X., and Jason Reynolds. *Stamped: Racism, Antiracism, and You.* New York: Little, Brown Books for Young Readers, 2020.

"Kala Bagai—Timeline," South Asian American Digital Archive. www.saada.org/project/timeline/kala-bagai.

"Largest U.S. Immigrant Groups over Time, 1960–Present,"

Migration Policy Institute Data Hub. www.migrationpolicy.org /programs/data-hub/charts/largest-immigrant-groups-over -time.

Lee, Christa. "5 People and Events That Changed Asian American LGBTQ+ History," Sunday Edit, August 20, 2021, edit .sundayriley.com/5-people-and-events-that-changed-asian -american-lgbtq-history.

Lee, Grace. *K-Town'92*, ktown92.com.

Lee, Mary Paik. *Quiet Odyssey: A Pioneer Korean Woman in America*, ed. Sucheng Chan. Seattle: University of Washington Press, 2019.

"Luce-Celler Act of 1946," The University of Texas at Austin, Immigration History. immigrationhistory.org/item/luce-celler-act.

Mabalon, Dawn Bohulano. "Mabuhay Ang Causa! The Stockton Connection to the Delano Grape Strike and the United Farm Workers," Little Manila. littlemanila.org/stockton-connection -to-delano-grape-strike.

Maeda, Daryl Joji. *Like Water: A Cultural History of Bruce Lee.* New York: New York University Press, 2022.

"Major Events of the Cold War," C-Span Classroom, November 3, 2017. www.c-span.org/classroom/document/?7342.

"May 19, 1921: Yuri Kochiyama Born," Zinn Education Project. www.zinnedproject.org/news/tdih/yuri-kochiyama-was-born.

Maze, Jonathan. "For Many Immigrants, Restaurants Are the American Dream," Nation's Restaurant News, March 29, 2017. www.nrn.com/franchising/many-immigrants-restaurants -are-american-dream.

"Medal of Honor Recipient Daniel Inouye Led a Life of Service to His Country," The National WWII Museum, July 19, 2020. www.nationalww2museum.org/war/articles/medal-of-honor-recipient-daniel-inouye.

"Military Intelligence Service," Go for Broke National Education Center. goforbroke.org/military-intelligence-service.

Mink, Gwendolyn, and Judy Tzu-Chun Wu. *Fierce and Fearless: Patsy Takemoto Mink, First Woman of Color in Congress.* New York: New York University Press, 2022.

"Mohini Bhardwaj," OOA Gymnastics. www.ooagymnastics.com/trainers/mohini-bhardwaj.

National Geographic Society, "Oct 12, 1492 CE: Columbus Makes Landfall in the Caribbean." www.nationalgeographic.org/thisday/oct12/columbus-makes-landfall-caribbean.

"Nationality Act of 1790," The University of Texas at Austin, Immigration History. immigrationhistory.org/item/1790-nationality-act.

"New Jersey High School Students Win Fight to Require Asian-American History in Curriculum," CBS News, February 4, 2022. www.cbsnews.com/newyork/news/new-jersey-asian-american-aapi-history-school-curriculum.

Ngai, Mae. *The Lucky Ones: One Family and the Extraordinary Invention of Chinese America.* New Jersey: Princeton University Press, 2012.

Nghiem, An, and Peggy Rowe Ward. "When Giants Meet," Thich Nhat Hanh Foundation, January 11, 2017. thichnhathanhfoundation.org/blog/2017/8/9/when-giants-meet.

"Our Stories: An Introduction to South Asian America," South Asian American Digital Archive, 2022.

PBS. "The Middle Passage." www.pbs.org/wgbh/aia/part1/1p277 .html.

Peele, Holly, and Maya Riser-Kositsky. "Statistics on School Sports: How Many Students Play Sports? Which Sports Do They Play?," *Education Week*, September 28, 2022. www.edweek .org/leadership/statistics-on-school-sports-how-many-students -play-sports-which-sports-do-they-play/2021/07.

Pokotylo, Katia. "Downtown Berkeley Street Renamed after South Asian Immigrant Kala Bagai," *Daily Californian*, February 11, 2021.

Ramakrishnan, Karthick. "How 1965 Changed Asian America, in 2 graphs," AAPI Data, September 28, 2015. aapidata.com /blog/1965-two-graphs.

"Rani Bagai on 'Vaishno Das Bagai,'" South Asian American Digital Archive. www.saada.org/item/20130821-3099.

"Repeal of Chinese Exclusion (1943)," The University of Texas at Austin, Immigration History. immigrationhistory.org /item/1943-repeal of chinese-exclusion.

Reuters Staff. "Chronology—Who Banned Slavery When?," Reuters, March 22, 2007. www.reuters.com/article/uk-slavery/chronology -who-banned-slavery-when-idUSL1561464920070322.

"Rhineland Campaign: Rescue of the Lost Battalion," Go for Broke National Education Center. goforbroke.org/rhineland -campaign-rescue-of-the-lost-battalion.

"Richard Nixon Statement on Signing the Education Amendments of 1972," The American Presidency Project, UC Santa Barbara. www.presidency.ucsb.edu/documents/statement-signing-the -education-amendments-1972.

Rutherford, Adam. "A New History of the First Peoples in the Americas," *The Atlantic*, October 3, 2017. www.theatlantic .com/science/archive/2017/10/a-brief-history-of-everyone-who -ever-lived/537942.

Ryerson, Jade. "Yuri Kochiyama," National Park Service, June 17, 2021. www.nps.gov/people/yuri-kochiyama.htm.

See Us Unite Video Project. www.youtube.com/@seeusunite6033 /videos.

"Sen. Daniel Inouye on Pearl Harbor, After 70 Years," *Tell Me More*, NPR News, December 7, 2011. www.npr.org/2011 /12/07/143271323/sen-daniel-inouye-on-pearl-harbor-after -70-years.

SlaveVoyages Database, "Trans-Atlantic Slave Trade—Estimates." www.slavevoyages.org/assessment/estimates.

Singh, Simran Jeet. *The Light We Give: How Sikh Wisdom Can Transform Your Life*. New York: Riverhead Books, 2022.

Sone, Monica. *Nisei Daughter*. Seattle: University of Washington Press, 2014.

Tajima-Peña, Renee (prod.). *Asian Americans*, PBS, 2020.

Takei, Barbara. "Tule Lake," Densho Encyclopedia. encyclopedia .densho.org/Tule_Lake.

"The Caribbean East Indians, Part 1 of 2," CaribNation TV, YouTube video. www.youtube.com/watch?v=oxFrQd6lVzA.

"The Doctrine of Discovery, 1493," The Gilder Lehrman Institute

of American History, www.gilderlehrman.org/history-resources
/spotlight-primary-source/doctrine-discovery-1493.

"The Origins of the Cold War, 1945–1949," National Endowment
for the Humanities: EDSITEment. edsitement.neh.gov/curricula
/origins-cold-war-1945-1949.

"The Philippine-American War: 1899–1902," US Department of State Office of the Historian. history.state.gov
/milestones/1899-1913/war.

"The State of The World's Refugees 2000: Fifty Years of Humanitarian Action—Chapter 4: Flight from Indochina," The UN
Refugee Agency. www.unhcr.org/3ebf9bad0.html.

Thomas, Heather. "Before *Brown v. Board of Education*,
There Was *Tape v. Hurley*," *Headlines and Heroes* (blog),
Library of Congress Blogs, May 5, 2021. blogs.loc.gov
/headlinesandheroes/2021/05/before-brown-v-education-there
-was-tape-v-hurley.

Thompson, Daniella. "The Tapes of Russell Street," Berkeley
Architectural Heritage Association, April 30, 2004. berkeley
heritage.com/essays/tape_family.html.

Tom, Pamela. "Tyrus," *American Masters*, season 31, episode 7,
PBS, 2017, www.pbs.org/wnet/americanmasters/tyrus-wong
-biography/9197.

Treuer, Anton. *Everything You Wanted to Know About Indians
But Were Afraid to Ask: Young Readers Edition*. New York:
Levine Querido Books, 2021.

"Tuck Pride and Tuck News Hour Hosted Guest Speakers," Tuck
School of Business at Dartmouth. www.tuck.dartmouth.edu

/news/articles/tuck-pride-and-tuck-news-hour-to-host-guest-speakers-on-may-1.

Tumin, Remy. "Fifty Years On, Title IX's Legacy Includes Its Durability," *New York Times*, June 23, 2022. www.nytimes.com/2022/06/23/sports/title-ix-anniversary.html.

"Unit History: 100th Infantry Battalion" and "Unit History: 442nd Regimental Combat Team," Go for Broke National Education Center. goforbroke.org/history/unit-history.

"Unit History: Japanese American Women in Service," Go For Broke National Education Center. goforbroke.org/history/unit-history/japanese-american-women-in-service.

"Vietnam War U.S. Military Fatal Casualty Statistics," US National Archives. www.archives.gov/research/military/vietnam-war/casualty-statistics.

von Oldershausen, Sasha. "How Growing Up in New York After 9/11 Shaped These Muslim Leaders," *New York Times*, September 11, 2021. www.nytimes.com/2021/09/10/nyregion/sept-11-muslim-new-york.html.

"What Was the Great Depression?," Franklin D. Roosevelt Presidential Library and Museum. www.fdrlibrary.org/great-depression-facts.

Wool-Rim Sjöblom, Lisa. *Palimpsest: Documents from a Korean Adoption*. Montreal: Drawn and Quarterly, 2019.

Wong, Kent. "United Farm Workers (UFW) Movement: Philip Vera Cruz, Unsung Hero," UCLA Asian American Studies Center. www.aasc.ucla.edu/resources/untoldstories/UCRS_Philip_Vera_Cruz_r2.pdf.

Yam, Kimmy. "Anti-Asian Hate Crimes Increased 339 Percent Nationwide Last Year, Report Says," NBC News, January 31, 2022. www.nbcnews.com/news/asian-america /anti-asian-hate-crimes-increased-339-percent-nationwide-last -year-repo-rcna14282.

Yang, Jeff. "'Oriental': Rugs, Not People." By Linda Wertheimer. *Tell Me More*, NPR, September 2, 2009. www.npr.org/templates /story/story.php?storyId=112465167.

Yang, Kao Kalia. *The Latehomecomer: A Hmong Family Memoir*. Minneapolis: Coffee House Press, 2008.

Yoo, Paula. *From a Whisper to a Rallying Cry: The Killing of Vincent Chin and the Trial That Galvanized the Asian American Movement*. New York: Norton Young Readers, 2021.

Zia, Helen, and the Vincent Chin Institute. "The Vincent Chin Legacy Guide: Asian Americans and Civil Rights," 2022.

Zhou, Kyler. "The Sinophobia Outbreak." *Hear Our Voices*, December 13, 2020.

IMAGE CREDITS

INTRODUCTION

Credit: Courtesy of Yifeng Hu

Photo by Alexi Rosenfeld/Getty Images

WHO ARE ASIAN AMERICANS?

Pew Research Center

CHAPTER 1: COLUMBUS'S MISTAKE

Theodor de Bry, Reisen im Occidentalischen Indien, vol. 2 (Franck-fort am Mayn: s.n., 1594–1597). Courtesy of the James Ford Bell Library, University of Minnesota.

Source: Bry, Theodor de, Antonio de Herrera y Tordesillas, Johann Theodor de Huth, Henry Acosta, José de Turnbull, Huth, Henry, and Bernard Quaritch bookseller. Noui orbis pars duodecima., Sive, Descriptio Indiae occidentalis, / auctore Antonio de Herrera, supremo castellae & Indiarum authoritate Philippi III. Hispaniarum regis historigrapho. Accesserunt et aliorum Indiae Occidentalis descriptiones, vti & nauigationum ominium per Fregum Magellicaum succincta narratio. Quibus cohaerent, Paralipomena Americae, in quibus res plurimae memoria & obseruatione dignissimae, imprimis regionum natura, aeris constitutio, temperamenta elementorum, incolarum ingenia quae in magno opere historico aut omittuntur aut leuiter attinguntur, iucunda non minus quam erudita descriptione pertractantur. Francofurti: Sumptibus haeredum Iohan. Theodori de Bry., 1624.

CHAPTER 2: FOLLOWING THE ROUTES OF EMPIRE: ASIANS IN "NEW SPAIN"

Abraham Ortelius, Theatrum orbis terrarum (His Epitome of the Theater of the World) (London, Ieames Shawe, 1603). Courtesy of the James Ford Bell Library, University of Minnesota.
Charles L. Thompson Collection, Mss. 998, Louisiana and Lower Mississippi Valley Collections, LSU Libraries, Baton Rouge, Lousiana.

CHAPTER 3: BROKEN PROMISES: AFONG MOY AND THE STRUGGLES OF ASIAN LABORERS

New York Public Library
Courtesy of Mount Vernon Ladies' Association
"Preserving the Peace," Harper's New Monthly Magazine 29 (June 1864) p. 5.

WHAT'S IN A NAME?

Seattle Daily Times, April 19, 1900, p. 8.
"Die Gelbe Gefahr," (the "Yellow Peril") reproduced in Review of Reviews (London), December 12, 1895.

CHAPTER 4: IN SEARCH OF GOLD MOUNTAIN: MAMIE TAPE AND THE FIRST CHINESE IN AMERICA

Beinecke Rare Book and Manuscript Library, Yale University Library.

Genthe photograph collection, Library of Congress, Prints and Photographs Division.

The Bancroft Library, University of California, Berkeley.

Courtesy of Jack Kim

CHAPTER 5: ONE THOUSAND QUESTIONS: TYRUS WONG, ANGEL ISLAND, AND CHINESE EXCLUSION

National Archives at College Park—Still Pictures

Library of Congress

National Archives at College Park—Still Pictures

Courtesy of the National Archives at San Francisco

WHO GETS TO BE AN AMERICAN?

Courtesy of the National Archives at San Francisco

The Rubel Collection, Gift of William Rubel, 2001 Accession Number: 2001.756; The Metropolitan Museum of Art

CHAPTER 6: UNWAVERING: MARY PAIK LEE

Courtesy of University of Southern California, on behalf of the USC Libraries Special Collections.

Courtesy of University of Southern California, on behalf of the USC Libraries Special Collections.

Courtesy of University of Southern California, on behalf of the USC Libraries Special Collections.

CHAPTER 7: STEADFAST SURVIVORS: THE BAGAI FAMILY

Vaishno Das and Kala Bagai Family Materials. South Asian American Digital Archive.

Vaishno Das and Kala Bagai Family Materials. South Asian American Digital Archive.

South Asian American Digital Archive.

South Asian American Digital Archive.

CHAPTER 8: AN ALL-AMERICAN GIRL: MONICA ITOI SONE

Courtesy of Hanover College Archives, MSS 1_Box7_125.

Frank and Frances Carpenter Collection, Library of Congress.

Wing Luke Asian Museum Photograph Collection / Creative Commons Attribution 2.0 Generic

San Francisco Chronicle, March 9, 1905

CHAPTER 9: ALREADY AMERICAN: FRANCISCO CARIÑO

Filipino American National Historic Society

Library of Congress

The Bancroft Library. University of California, Berkeley

Library of Congress

CHAPTER 10: MILITARY NECESSITY: THE INCARCERATION OF JAPANESE AMERICANS

US National Archives and Records Administration

Dr. Seuss Collection, Special Collections & Archives, UC San Diego

Records of the War Relocation Authority

US National Archives and Records Administration

AMERICA'S CONCENTRATION CAMPS
US National Archives and Records Administration
US National Archives and Records Administration
Library of Congress
The Bancroft Library. University of California, Berkeley
Corbis Historical / Getty Images

CHAPTER 11: "GOOD" ASIANS, "BAD" ASIANS
US Government Printing Office
Library of Congress
Franklin D. Roosevelt Presidential Library and Museum
Courtesy of Cuddy Family Archives
Time, December, 22, 1941

CHAPTER 12: LOYALTY
Courtesy of Robert and Elizabeth Dole Archive and Special Collections
US National Archives and Records Administration
Courtesy of the Fred T. Korematsu Institute
US Department of Defense / DVIDS (United States Holocaust Memorial Museum photo courtesy of Eric Saul)

CHAPTER 13: IMPOSSIBLE DREAMS: DEANN BORSHAY
Courtesy of Deann Borshay
Map by HarperCollins

US National Archives and Records Administration

Photo by John Chillingworth/Picture Post/Hulton Archive/Getty Images

FROM PICTURE BRIDES TO PUNK ROCKERS: ASIAN AMERICAN WOMEN MAKE HISTORY

Courtesy of California State Parks, Number 090-544

Photo by Monica Schipper/Getty Images for Netflix

Stefan Brending, Lizenz

CHAPTER 14: SOLIDARITY: THE ONGOING FIGHT FOR CIVIL RIGHTS

Japanese American National Museum (Gift of Mrs. Yuri Kochiyama, 96.42.6)

Courtesy of Corky Lee Estate

Courtesy of Walter P. Reuther Library, Archives of Labor and Urban Affairs, Wayne State University

CHAPTER 15: AMERICA'S GATES REOPEN: THE 1965 IMMIGRATION AND NATIONALITY ACT

Courtesy of Wendy Chou Le

Courtesy of LBJ Presidential Library

Pew Research Center, "Key Facts About Asian Origin Groups in the US," 2021.

Courtesy of Christina Soontornvat

ASIAN AMERICAN FOOD

Drew Arrieta, Sahan Journal

Courtesy of Erika Lee
Courtesy of Christina Soontornvat

CHAPTER 16: THE MYTHICAL MODEL MINORITY

Photo by Bettmann Archive/Getty Images
Time Magazine
"Key Facts About Asian Origin Groups in the U.S." Pew Research
Center, Washington, DC. (2021), www.pewresearch.org/short
-reads/2021/04/29/key-facts-about-asian-origin-groups-in
-the-u-s/.

CHAPTER 17: FIRSTS AND FLYING FISTS

Archive Photos/Moviepix/Getty Images
Certificate of Identity Issues to Actress Anna May Wong, 1924.
    US National Archives and Records Administration
Patsy T. Mink Papers at the Library of Congress
Courtesy of Helen Zia
Washington Blade photo by Michael Key
Sammy Lee/Vickie Draves: FPG/Archive Photos/Getty Images
Wataru Misaka: Bettmann/U.P.I.
Mohini Bhardwaj: J. Bierbaum
Tiger Woods: Jamie Squire/Getty Images

CHAPTER 18: SEEKING REFUGE: SOUTHEAST ASIAN AMERICANS

Photo by Maja Hitij/Getty Images
Bettmann
Associated Press

Minnesota Historical Society

Photo courtesy of the Yang Family

CHAPTER 19: "IT'S BECAUSE OF YOU"–THE MURDER OF VINCENT CHIN

Copyright © 2024 Helen Zia

Copyright © 2024 Helen Zia

CHAPTER 20: LEFT TO BURN: KOREATOWN ON SA I GU

© 1992 Hyungwon Kang

© 1992 Hyungwon Kang

AP Images / David Longstreath

CHAPTER 21: "LOOKING LIKE THE ENEMY"

Courtesy of Simran Jeet Singh

Photo by Don Bartletti/*Los Angeles Times* via Getty Images

Lorie Shaull

Rhododendrites, CC BY-SA 4.0 <creativecommons.org/licenses /by-sa/4.0>, via Wikimedia Commons

CHAPTER 22: ASIAN AMERICAN RECKONINGS

Andrew Ratto from Berkeley, USA, CC BY 2.0 <creativecommons .org/licenses/by/2.0>, via Wikimedia Commons

CHAPTER 23: MADE IN ASIAN AMERICA

Courtesy of Erika Lee

Courtesy of Yifeng Hu

INDEX